Days of Heaven Upon Earth

by

A.B. Simpson

THE DAYS OF HEAVEN

The days of heaven are peaceful days,
Still as yon glassy sea;
So calm, so still in God, our days,
As the days of heaven would be.
The days of heaven are holy days,
From sin forever free;
So cleansed and kept our days, O Lord,
As the days of heaven would be.
The days of heaven are happy days.
Sorrow they never see;
So full of gladness all our days,
As the days of heaven would be.
The days of heaven are healthful days,
They feed on life's fair tree;
So feeding on Thy strength, O Christ,
Our days as heaven may be.
Walk with us, Lord, thro' all the days,
And let us walk with Thee;
Till as Thy will is done in heaven,
On earth so shall it be.

JANUARY 1.

"Redeeming the time" (Eph. v. 16).

Two little words are found in the Greek version here. They are translated "_ton kairon_" in the revised version, "Buying up for yourselves the opportunity." The two words _ton kairon_ mean, literally, the opportunity.

They do not refer to time in general, but to a special point of time, a juncture, a crisis, a moment full of possibilities and quickly passing by, which we must seize and make the best of before it has passed away.

It is intimated that there are not many such moments of opportunity, because the days are evil; like a barren desert, in which, here and there, you find a flower, pluck it while you can; like a business opportunity which comes a few times in a life-time; buy it up while you have the chance. Be spiritually alert; be not unwise, but understanding what the will of God is. "Walk circumspectly, not as fools, but as wise, buying up for yourselves the opportunity."

Sometimes it is a moment of time to be saved; sometimes a soul to be led to Christ; sometimes it is an occasion for love; sometimes for patience: sometimes for victory over temptation and sin. Let us redeem it.

JANUARY 2.

"I will cause you to walk in My statutes" (Eze. xxxvi. 27).

The highest spiritual condition is one where life is spontaneous and flows without effort, like the deep floods of Ezekiel's river, where the struggles of the swimmer ceased, and he was borne by the current's resistless force.

So God leads us into spiritual conditions and habits which become the spontaneous impulses of our being, and we live and move in the fulness of the divine life.

But these spiritual habits are not the outcome of some transitory impulse, but are often slowly acquired and established. They begin, like every true habit, in a definite act of will, and they are confirmed by the repetition of that act until it becomes a habit. The first stages always involve effort and choice. We have to take a stand and hold it steadily, and after we have done so a certain time, it becomes second nature, and carries us by its own force.

The Holy Spirit is willing to form such habits in every direction of our Christian life, and if we will but obey Him in the first steppings of faith, we will soon become established in the attitude of obedience, and duty will be delight.

JANUARY 3.

"Watch and pray" (Matt. xxvi. 41).

We need to watch for prayers as well as for the answers to our prayers. It needs as much wisdom to pray rightly as it does faith to receive the answers to our prayers.

We met a friend the other day, who had been in years of darkness because God had failed to answer certain prayers, and the result had been a state bordering on infidelity.

A very few moments were sufficient to convince this friend that these prayers had been entirely unauthorized, and that God had never promised to answer such prayers, and they were for things which this friend should have accomplished himself, in the exercise of ordinary wisdom.

The result was deliverance from a cloud of unbelief which was almost wrecking a Christian life. There are some things about which we do not need to pray, as much as to take the light which God has already given.

Many persons are asking God to give them peculiar signs, tokens and supernatural intimations of His will. Our business is to use the light He has given, and then He will give whatever more we need.

JANUARY 4.

"Blessed is the man that walketh not" (Ps. i. 1).

Three things are notable about this man:

1. His company. "He walketh not in the counsel of the ungodly, nor standeth in the way of sinners, nor sitteth in the seat of the scornful."
2. His reading and thinking. "His delight is in the law of the Lord, and in His law doth he meditate day and night."
3. His fruitfulness. "And he shall be like a tree planted by the rivers of water, that bringeth forth his fruit in his season; his leaf also shall not wither, and whatsoever he doeth shall prosper."

The river is the Holy Ghost; the planting, the deep, abiding life in which, not occasionally, but habitually, we absorb the Holy Spirit; and the fruit is not occasional, but continual, and appropriate to each changing season.

His life is also prosperous, and his spirit fresh, like the unfading leaf. Such a life must be happy. Indeed, happiness is a matter of spiritual conditions. Put a sunbeam in a cellar and it must be bright. Put a nightingale in the darkest midnight, and it must sing.

JANUARY 5.

"I know him that he will do the law" (Gen. xviii. 19).

God wants people that He can depend upon. He could say of Abraham, "I know him, that the Lord may bring upon Abraham all that He hath spoken." God can be depended upon; He wants us to be just as decided, as reliable, as stable. This is just what faith means. God is looking for men on whom He can put the weight of all His love, and power, and faithful promises. When God finds such a soul there is nothing He will not do for him. God's engines are strong enough to draw any weight we attach to them. Unfortunately the cable which we fasten to the engine is often too weak to hold the weight of our prayer, therefore God is drilling us, disciplining us, and training us to stability and certainty in the life of faith. Let us learn our lessons, and let us stand fast.

God has His best things for the few
Who dare to stand the test;
God has his second choice for those
Who will not have His best.

Give me, O Lord, Thy highest choice,
Let others take the rest.
Their good things have no charm for me,
For I have got Thy best.

JANUARY 6.

"The body is not one member, but many" (I. Cor. xii. 14).

We have a friend who has a phonograph for his correspondence. It consists of two parts. One is a simple and wonderful apparatus, whose sensitive cylinders receive the tones and then give them out again, word for word, through the hearing tube. The other part is a common little box that stands under the table, and does nothing but supply the power through connecting wires.

Now, the little box might insist upon being the phonograph, and doing the talking; but if it should, it would not only waste its own life but destroy the life of its partner.

Its sole business is to supply power to the phonograph, while the latter is to do the talking. So some of us are called to be voices to speak for God to our fellow-men, others are forces to sustain them, by our holy sympathy and silent prayer. (Some of us are little dynamos under the table, while others are phonographs that speak aloud the messages of heaven.)

Let each of us be true to our God-given ministry, and when the day comes our work will be weighed and the rewards distributed.

JANUARY 7.

"Now unto Him that is able to keep you from stumbling" (Jude 24).

This is a most precious promise. The revised translation is both accurate and suggestive. It is not merely from falling that He wants to keep us, but from even the slightest stumbling.

We are told of Abraham that he staggered not at the promise. God wants us to walk so steadily that there will not even be a quiver in the line of His regiments as they face the foe. It is the little stumblings of life that most discourage and hinder us, and most of these stumblings are over trifles. Satan would much rather knock us down with a feather than with an Armstrong gun. It is much more to his honor and keen delight to defeat a child of God by some flimsy trifle than by some great temptation.

Beloved, let us watch, in these days, against the orange peels that trip us on our pathway, the little foxes that destroy the vines, and the dead flies that mar, sometimes, a whole vessel of precious ointment. "Trifles make perfection," and as we get farther on, in our Christian life, God will hold us much more closely to obedience in things that seem insignificant.

JANUARY 8.

"It is I, be not afraid" (Mark vi. 50).

Someone tells of a little child with some big story of sorrow upon its little heart, flying to its mother's arms for comfort, and intending to tell her the story of its trouble; but as that mother presses it to her bosom and pours out her love, it soon becomes so occupied with her and the sweetness of her affection that it

10

forgets to tell its story, and in a little while even the memory of the trouble is forgotten. It has just been loved away, and she has taken its place in the heart of the little one.

This is the way God comforts us Himself. "It is I, be not afraid," is His reassuring word. The circumstances are not altered, but He Himself comes in their place, and satisfies every need of our being, and we forget all things in His sweet presence, as He becomes our all in all.

I am breathing out my sorrow
On Thy kind and loving breast;
Breathing in Thy joy and comfort,
Breathing in Thy peace and rest.

I am breathing out my longings
In Thy listening, loving ear;
I am breathing in Thy answer,
Stilling every doubt and fear.

JANUARY 9.

"Not as I will, but as Thou wilt" (Matt. xxvi. 39).

"To will and do of His good pleasure" (Phil. ii. 13).

There are two attitudes in which our will should be given to God.

First. We should have the surrendered will. This is where we must all begin, by yielding up to God our natural will, and having Him possess it.

But next, He wants us to have the victorious will. As soon as He receives our will in honest surrender, He wants to put His will into it and make it stronger than ever for Him. It is henceforth no longer our will, but His will. And having yielded to His choice and placed itself under His direction, He wants to put into it all the strength and intensity of His own great will and make us positive, forceful, victorious and unmovable, even as Himself. "Not My will, but Thine be done." That is the first step. "Father, I will that they whom Thou hast given Me, be with Me." That is the second attitude. Both are divine; both are right; both are necessary to our right living and successful working for God.

JANUARY 10.

"Charity doth not behave itself unseemly" (I. Cor. xiii. 5).

In the dress of a Hindu woman, her graceful robe is fastened upon her person entirely by means of a single knot. The long strip of cloth is wound around her person so as to fall in graceful folds like a made garment, and the end is fastened by a little knot, and the whole thing hangs by that single fastening. If that were loosed the robe would fall. And so in the spiritual life, our habits of grace are likened unto garments; and it is also true that the garment of love, which is the beautiful adorning of the child of God, is entirely fastened by little _nots_.

If you will read with care the thirteenth chapter of I. Corinthians, you will find that most of the qualities of love are purely negative. "Love envieth not, love vaunteth not itself, is not puffed up, doth not behave herself rudely, seeketh not her own, is not provoked, thinketh no evil." Here are "_nots_" enough to hold on our spiritual wardrobe. Here are reasons enough to explain the failure of so many, and the reason why they walk naked, or with rent garments, and others see their shame. Let us look after the _nots_.

JANUARY 11.

"Hold fast till I come" (Rev. ii. 25).

The other day we asked a Hebrew friend how it was that his countrymen were so successful in acquiring wealth. "Ah," said he, "we do not make more money than other people, but we keep more." Beloved, let us look out this day for spiritual pickpockets and spiritual leakage. Let us "lose nothing of what we have wrought, but receive a full reward"; and, as each day comes and goes, let us put away in the savings bank of eternity its treasures of grace and victory, and so be conscious from day to day that something real and everlasting is being added to our eternal fortune.

It may be but a little, but if we only economize all that God gives us, and pass it on to His keeping, when the close shall come we shall be amazed to see how much the accumulated treasures of a well spent life have laid up on high, and how much more He has added to them by His glorious investment of the life committed to His keeping.

Oh, how the days are telling! Oh, how precious these golden hours will seem sometime! God help us to make the most of them now.

JANUARY 12.

"Ask and it shall be given you" (Matt. vii. 7).

12

We must receive, as well as ask. We must take the place of believing, and recognize ourselves as in it. A friend was saying, "I want to get into the will of God," and this was the answer: "Will you step into the will of God? And now, are you in the will of God?" The question aroused a thought that had not come before.

The gentleman saw that he had been straining after, but not receiving the blessing he sought.

Jesus has said, "Ask and ye shall receive." The very strain keeps back the blessing. The intense tension of all your spiritual nature so binds you that you are not open to the blessing which God is waiting to give you. "Whosoever will, let him take the water of life freely."

He tells me there is cleansing
From every secret sin,
And a great and full salvation
To keep the heart within.
And I take Him in His fulness,
With all His glorious grace,
For He says it is mine by taking,
And I take just what He says.

JANUARY 13.

"Thou shalt be to him instead of God" (Ex. iv. 16).

Such was God's promise to Moses, and such the high character that Moses was to assume toward Aaron, his brother. May it not suggest a high and glorious place that each of us may occupy toward all whom we meet, instead of God?

What a dignity and glory it would give our lives, could we uniformly realize this high calling! How it would lead us to act toward our fellow-men! God can always be depended upon. God is without variableness or shadow of turning. God's word is unchangeable, and we can trust Him without reserve or question. Oh, that we might so live that men can trust us, even as God!

Again, God has no needs or wants to be supplied. He is always giving. "Rich unto all that call upon Him." The glory of His nature is love, unselfish love, and beneficence toward all His creatures. The Divine life is a self-forgetting life, a life that has nothing to do but love and bless.

13

Let us so live, representing our Master here, while He represents us before the Throne on high.

JANUARY 14.

"Unto the measure of the stature of the fulness of Christ" (Eph. iv. 13).

God loves us so well that He will not suffer us to take less than His highest will. Some day we shall bless our faithful teacher, who kept the standard inflexibly rigid, and then gave us the strength and grace to reach it, and would not excuse us until we had accomplished all His glorious will.

Let us be inexorable with ourselves. Let us mean exactly what God means, and have no discounts upon His promises or commandments. Let us keep the standard up, and never rest until we reach it. "Let God be true and every man a liar." If we fail a hundred times don't let us accommodate God's ideal to our realization, but like the brave ensign who stood in front of his company waving the banner, and when the soldiers called him back he only waved it higher, and cried, "Don't bring the standard back to the regiment, but bring the regiment up to the colors."

Forward, forward, leave the past behind thee,

Reaching forth unto the things before;

All the Land of Promise lies before thee,

God has greater blessings yet in store.

JANUARY 15.

"As ye have received Christ Jesus so walk in Him" (Col. ii. 6).

It is much easier to keep the fire burning than to rekindle it after it has gone out. Let us abide in Him. Let us not have to remove the cinders and ashes from our hearthstones every day and kindle a new flame; but let us keep it burning and never let it expire. Among the ancient Greeks the sacred fire was never allowed to go out; so, in a higher sense, let us keep the heavenly flame aglow upon the altar of the heart.

It takes very much less effort to maintain a good habit than to form it. A true spiritual habit once formed becomes a spontaneous tendency of our being, and we grow into delightful freedom in following it. "Let us not be ever laying again the foundation of repentance from dead works, but let us go on unto perfection;

14

and whereto we have already attained, let us walk by the same rule, let us mind the same things."

Every spiritual habit begins with difficulty and effort and watchfulness, but if we will only let it get thoroughly established, it will become a channel along which currents of life will flow with divine spontaneousness and freedom.

JANUARY 16.

"Prove what is that good, and acceptable and perfect will of God" (Rom. xii. 2).

There are three conditions in which the water in that engine may be. First, the boiler may be full and the water clean and clear; or, secondly, the boiler may not only be full but the water may be hot, very hot, hot enough to scald you, almost boiling; thirdly, it may be just one degree hotter and at the boiling point, giving forth its vapor in clouds of steam, pressing through the valves and driving the mighty piston which turns the wheels and propels the train of cars across the country.

So there are three kinds of Christians. The first we will call cold water Christians, or, perhaps better, clean water Christians.

Secondly, there are hot water Christians. They are almost at the boiling point.

One degree more, we come to the third class of Christians, the boiling water Christians. The difference is a very slight one; it simply takes one reservation out, drops one "if," eliminates a single touch, and yet it is all the difference in the world. That one degree changes that engine into a motive power, not now a thing to be looked at, but a thing to go.

JANUARY 17.

"It is God which worketh in you" (Phil. ii. 13).

God has not two ways for any of us; but one; not two things for us to do which we may choose between; but one best and highest choice. It is a blessed thing to find and fill the perfect will of God. It is a blessed thing to have our life laid out and our Christian work adjusted to God's plan. Much strength is lost by working at a venture. Much spiritual force is expended in wasted effort, and scattered, indefinite and inconstant attempts at doing good. There is spiritual force and financial strength enough in the hands and hearts of the consecrated Christians of to-day to bring the coming of Christ, to bring about the evangelization of the world in a generation, if it were only wisely directed and utilized according to God's plan.

Christ has laid down a definite plan of work for His Church, and He expects us to understand it, and to work up to it; and as we catch His thought, and obediently, loyally fulfil it, we shall work to purpose, and please Him far better than by our thoughtless, reckless, and indiscriminate attempts to carry out our ideas, and compel God to bless our work.

JANUARY 18.

"That take and give for Me and thee" (Matt. xvii. 27).

There is a beautiful touch of loving thoughtfulness in the account of Christ's miracle at Capernaum in providing the tribute money. After the reference to Peter's interview with the tax collector, it is added, "When he came into the house Jesus prevented him," that is, anticipated him, as the old Saxon word means, by arranging for the need before Peter needed to speak about it at all, and He sent Peter down to the sea to find the piece of gold in the mouth of the fish.

So our dear Lord is always thinking in advance of our needs, and He loves to save us from embarrassment, and anticipate our anxieties and cares by laying up His loving acts and providing before the emergency comes. Then with exquisite tenderness the Master adds: "That take and give for Me and thee." He puts Himself first in the embarrassing need and bears the heavy end of the burden for His distressed and suffering child. He makes our cares His cares, our sorrows His sorrows, our shame His shame, and "He is able to be touched with the feeling of our infirmities."

JANUARY 19.

"Prove me now herewith" (Mal. iii. 10).

We once heard a simple old colored man say something that we have never forgotten. "When God tests You it is a good time for you to test Him by putting His promises to the proof, and claiming from Him just as much as your trials have rendered necessary."

There are two ways of getting out of a trial. One is to simply try to get rid of the trial, and be thankful when it is over. The other is to recognize the trial as a challenge from God to claim a larger blessing than we have ever had, and to hail it with delight as an opportunity of obtaining a larger measure of Divine grace.

16

Thus even the adversary becomes an auxiliary, and the things that seem to be against us turn out to be for the furtherance of our way. Surely, this is to be more than conquerors through Him who loved us.

Blessed Rose of Sharon
Breathe upon our heart,
Fill us with Thy fragrance,
Keep us as Thou art.
Then Thy life will make us
Holy and complete;
In Thy grace triumphant,
In Thy sweetness, sweet.

JANUARY 20.

"Ye know not what manner of spirit ye are of" (Luke ix. 55).

Some one has said that the most spiritual people are the easiest to get along with. When one has a little of the Holy Ghost it is like "a little learning, a dangerous thing"; but a full baptism of the Holy Spirit, and a really disciplined, stablished and tested spiritual life, makes one simple, tender, tolerant, considerate of others, and like a little child.

James and John, in their early zeal, wanted to call down fire from heaven on the Samaritans. But John, the aged, allowed Demetrius to exclude him from the church, and suffered in Patmos for the kingdom and with the patience of Jesus. And aged Paul was willing to take back even Mark, whom he had refused as a companion in his early ministry, and to acknowledge that he was profitable to him for the ministry.

I want the love that cannot help but love;
Loving, like God, for very sake of love.
A spring so full that it must overflow,
A fountain flowing from the throne above.

"Now abideth faith, hope, love; but the greatest of these is love."

JANUARY 21.

"Pray without ceasing" (I. Thess. v. 17).

An important help in the life of prayer is the habit of bringing everything to God, moment by moment, as it comes to us in life. This may be established as a

17

habit on the principle on which all habits are formed, of repeated and constant attention, moment by moment, until that which is at first an act of will, becomes spontaneous and second nature.

If we will watch our lives we shall find that God meets the things that we commit to Him in prayer with special blessing, and often allows the best things that we have not committed to Him to be ineffectual, simply to remind us of our dependence upon Him for everything. It is very gracious and mindful of Him thus gently to compel us to remember Him and to hold us so close to Him that we cannot get away even the length of a single minute from His all-sustaining arm. "In everything ... let our requests be made known unto God."

Let us bring our least petitions,

Like the incense beaten small,

All our cares, complaints, conditions

Jesus loves to bear them all.

JANUARY 22.

"His wife hath made herself ready" (Rev. xix. 7).

There is danger in becoming morbid even in preparing for the Lord's coming. We remember a time in our life when we had devoted ourselves to spend a month in waiting upon the Lord for a baptism of the Holy Ghost, and before the end of the month, the Lord shook us out of our seclusion and compelled us to go out and carry His message to others; and as we went, He met us in the service.

There is a musty, monkish way of seeking a blessing, and there is a wholesome, practical holiness which finds us in the company of the Lord Himself not only in the closet and on the mountain-top of prayer, but among publicans and sinners, and in the practical duties of life.

It seems to us that the practical preparation for the Lord's coming consists, first, of a very full entering into fellowship with Him in our own spiritual life, and letting Him not only cleanse us, but perfect us in all the finer touches of the Spirit's deeper work, and then, secondly, getting out of ourselves and living for the help of others and the preparation of the world for His appearing.

JANUARY 23.

"I know a man in Christ" (II. Cor. xii. 2).

It is a great deliverance to lose one's self. There is no heavier millstone that one can be compelled to carry than self-consciousness. It is so easy to get introverted and coiled round one's self in our spiritual consciousness. There is nothing that is so easy to fasten on as our misery; there is nothing that is more apt to produce self-consciousness than suffering, until it becomes almost a settled habit to hold on to our burden, and pray it unceasingly into the very face of God, until our very prayer saturates us with our own misery, instead of asking for power to drop ourselves altogether, and leave ourselves in His loving hands and know that we are free, and then rise into the blessed liberty of His higher thoughts and will, and His love and care for others.

The very act of letting go of ourselves really lifts us into a higher plane, and relieves us from the thing that is hurting. This habit of prayer for others, and especially for the world, brings its own recompense, and leaves upon our hearts a blessing like the fertility which the Nile deposits upon the soil of Egypt, as it flows through to its distant goal.

JANUARY 24.

"Freely ye have received, freely give" (Matt. x. 8).

When God does anything marked and special for our souls, or bodies, He intends it as a sacred trust for us to communicate to others. "Freely ye have received, freely give."

It has pleased the Master in these closing days of the dispensation to reveal Himself in peculiar blessing to the hearts of His chosen disciples in all parts of the Christian Church; but this is intended to be communicated to a still wider circle, and every one of us who has been brought into these intimate relations with God, becomes a trustee, or witness for these higher truths to every one we can influence.

If God has revealed Himself to us as our Sanctifier, it is that we may help others to know Him as a Sanctifier.

If He has become our Healer, it is because there are sick and suffering lives to whom we can bring some blessing.

In like manner, if the hope of the Lord's coming has become precious to us, it would be worse than ingratitude for us to hide our testimony to this truth, and hold it only for our own personal comfort.

JANUARY 25.

"Hold fast that which is good" (I. Thess. v. 21).

It is a great thing to be able to receive new truth and blessing without sacrificing the truths already proved, and abandoning foundations already laid.

Some persons are always laying the foundations, and they present at last, the appearance of a lot of abandoned sites and half constructed buildings, and nothing is ever brought to completion.

The fact that you are abandoning to-day for some new truth the things that a year ago you counted most precious and believed to be divinely true, should be sufficient evidence that you will probably a year from to-day abandon your present convictions for the next new light that comes to you.

God is ever wanting to add to us, to develop us, to enlarge us, to teach us more and more, but it is ever in the line of things which He has already taught us, and in which we have been established.

While we are to "prove all things," let us "hold fast that which is good," and "whereto we have already attained, let us walk by the same rule, let us mind the same thing."

JANUARY 26.

"I called him alone and blessed him" (Isa. li. 2).

When we were in the East we noticed the beautiful process of raising rice. The rice is sown on a morass of mud and water, ploughed up by great buffaloes, and after a few weeks it springs up and appears above the water with its beautiful pale green shoots. The seed has been sown very thickly and the plants are clustered together in great numbers, so that you can pull up a score at a single handful. But now comes the process of transplanting. He first plants us and lets us grow very close to some of His children, and in great clusters in the nursery or the hothouse, but when we reach a certain stage we must be transplanted, or come to nothing. He calls us out by His Spirit and Providence into situations where we have to lean directly on Him, where He puts upon us a weight of responsibility and service so great that we have an opportunity of developing and are thrown upon the great resources of His grace.

"Blessed is the man that trusteth in the Lord, and whose hope the Lord is; for he shall be like a tree planted by the waters and that spreadeth out her roots by the rivers."

JANUARY 27.

"This one thing I do" (Phil. iii. 13).

One of Satan's favorite employees is the switchman. He likes nothing better than to side-track one of God's express trains, sent on some blessed mission and filled with the fire of a holy purpose.

Something will come up in the pathway of the earnest soul, to attract its attention and occupy its strength and thought. Sometimes it is a little irritation and provocation. Sometimes it is some petty grievance we stop to pursue or adjust. Sometimes it is somebody else's business in which we become interested, and which we feel bound to rectify, and before we know, we are absorbed in a lot of distracting cares and interests that quite turn us aside from the great purpose of our life.

Perhaps we do not do much harm, but we have missed our connection. We have got off the main line.

Let all these things alone. Let grievances come and go, but press forward steadily and irresistibly, crying, as you haste to the goal, "This one thing I do."

JANUARY 28.

"That my joy might remain in you, and that your joy might be full" (John xv. 11).

There is a joy that springs spontaneously in the heart without external or even rational cause. It is an artesian fountain. It rejoices because it cannot help it. It is the glory of God; it is the heart of Christ, it is the joy divine of which He says, "These things have I spoken unto you that My joy might remain in you, and that your joy might be full." And your joy no man taketh from you. He who possesses this fountain is not discouraged by surrounding circumstances, but is often surprised at the deep, sweet gladness that comes without any apparent cause, and even comes most strongly when everything in our condition and circumstances is fitted to fill us with sorrow and depression.

It is the nightingale in the heart, which sings at night, and sings because it is its nature to sing.

21

It is the glorified and incorruptible joy which belongs to heaven, and anticipates already the everlasting song. Lord, give me Thy joy under all circumstances this day, and let my full heart overflow in blessing to others.

JANUARY 29.

"Send portions unto them for whom nothing is prepared" (Neh. viii. 10).

That was a fine picture in the days of Nehemiah, when they were celebrating their glorious Feast of Tabernacles. "Neither be ye sorry; for the joy of the Lord is your strength. Go your way, eat the fat, and drink the sweet, and send portions to them for whom nothing is prepared."

How many there are on every side for whom nothing is prepared! Let us find out some sad and needy heart for whom there is no one else to think or care. Let us pray for some one that has none to pray for him. Let us be like Him who, one Christmas Day, gave His life and His all, and came to those who would not appreciate His holy gift, but rejected His blessed Babe, and murdered His only Son.

Let us not be afraid to know something even of the love that is unrequited and is thrown away on the unworthy. That is the love of Christ, and God has for such love a rich recompense.

How Christ must almost weep over the selfishness that meets Him from those for whom He died.

JANUARY 30.

"Cast down but not destroyed" (II. Cor. iv. 9).

How did God bring about the miracle of the Red Sea? By shutting His people in on every side, so that there was no way out but the divine way. The Egyptians were behind them, the sea was in front of them, the mountains were on every side of them. There was no escape but from above.

Some one has said that the devil can wall us in, but he cannot roof us over. We can always get out at the top. Our difficulties are but God's challenges, and He makes them so hard, often, that we must go under or get above them.

In such an hour, if there is a divine element, it brings out the highest possibilities of faith and we are pushed by the very emergency into God's best.

Beloved, this is God's hour. If you will rise to meet it you will get such a hold upon Him that you will never be in extremities again, or if you are, you will learn

22

to call them not extremities, but opportunities, and like Jacob, you will go forth from that night at Peniel, no longer Jacob, but victorious Israel. Let us bring to Him our need and prove Him true.

JANUARY 31.

"Jesus, who of God is made unto us wisdom, and righteousness and sanctification and redemption" (I. Cor. i. 30).

More and more we are coming to see the supreme importance of getting the right conception of sanctification, not as a blessing, but as a personal union with the personal Saviour and the indwelling Holy Spirit. Thousands of people get stranded after they have embarked on the great voyage of holiness.

They find themselves failing and falling, and are astonished and perplexed, and they conclude that they must have been mistaken in their experience, and so they make a new attempt at the same thing and again fall, until at last, worn out with the experiment, they conclude that the experience is a delusion, or, at least, that it was never intended for them, and so they fall back into the old way, and their last state is worse than their first.

What people need to-day to satisfy their deep hunger and to give them a permanent and Divine experience is to know, not sanctification as a state, but Christ as a living Person, who is waiting to enter the heart that is willing to receive Him.

FEBRUARY 1.

"A well of water springing up" (John iv. 14).

In the life overflowing in service for others, we find the deep fountain of life running over the spring and finding vent in rivers of living water that go out to bless and save the world around us. It is beautiful to notice that as the blessing grows unselfish it grows larger. The water in the heart is only a well, but when reaching out to the needs of others it is not only a river, but a delta of many rivers overflowing in majestic blessing. This overflowing love is connected with the Person and work of the Holy Spirit which was to be poured out upon the disciples after Jesus was glorified.

This is the true secret of power for service, the heart filled and satisfied with Jesus, and so baptized with the Holy Ghost that it is impelled by the fulness of its joy and love to impart to others what it has so abundantly received; and yet each

23

new ministry only makes room for a new filling and a deeper receiving of the life which grows by giving.

Letting go is twice possessing,
Would you double every blessing,
    Pass it on.

FEBRUARY 2.

"And whosoever will be great among you, let him be your minister. And whosoever will be chief among you, let him be your servant" (Matt. xx. 26, 27).

Slave is the literal meaning of the word, _doulos_.

The first word used for service is _diakanos_, which means a minister to others in any usual way or work: but the word _doulos_ means a bond slave, and the Lord here plainly teaches us that the highest service is that of a bond slave.

He Himself made Himself the servant of all, and he who would come nearest to Him and stand closest to Him at last, must likewise learn the spirit of the ministry that has utterly renounced selfish rights and claims forever.

It is quite possible to be entirely loyal to the Lord Jesus, and yet for Jesus' sake, a servant ourselves, and under the authority of those who are over us in the Lord.

The _doulos_ spirit is the spirit of self-renunciation and glad submission to proper authority, service utterly disinterested, yielding our own preferences and interests unreservedly for the glory of the Master and the sake of our brethren. Lord, clothe us with humility and make us wholly Thine.

FEBRUARY 3.

"He went out, not knowing whither He went" (Heb. xi. 8).

It is faith without sight. When we can see, it is not faith but reasoning. In crossing the Atlantic we observed this very principle of faith. We saw no path upon the sea nor sign of the shore. And yet day by day we were marking our path upon the chart as exactly as if there had followed us a great chalk line upon the sea; and when we came within twenty miles of land we knew where we were as exactly as if we had seen it all three thousand miles ahead.

How had we measured and marked our course? Day by day our captain had taken his instruments, and looking up to the sky had fixed his course by the sun. He was sailing by the heavenly, not the earthly lights. So faith looks up and sails

24

on, by God's great Sun, not seeing one shore line or earthly lighthouse or path upon the way. Often its steps seem to lead into utter uncertainty, and even darkness and disaster. But He opens the way, and often makes such midnight hours the very gates of day. Let us go forth this day, not knowing but trusting.

FEBRUARY 4.

"Lo, I am with you alway" (Matt. xxviii. 20).

This living Christ is not the person that was, but the person that still is, your living Lord. At Preston Pans, near Edinburgh, I looked on the field where in the olden days armies were engaged in contest. In the crisis of the battle the chieftain fell wounded. His men were about to shrink away from the field when they saw their leader's form go down; their strong hands held the claymore with trembling grip, and they faltered for a moment. Then the old chieftain rallied strength enough to rise on his elbow and cry: "I am not dead, my children, I am only watching you--to see my clansmen do their duty." And so from the other side of Calvary He is speaking; we cannot see Him, but He says, "Lo, I am with you alway, even to the end of the world"; and He puts it, "I am"--an uninterrupted and continuous presence. Not "I will be," but the unbroken presence still is with us forevermore.

Soon the conflict shall be done,
Soon the battle shall be won;
Soon shall wave the victor's palm,
Soon shall sing the eternal Psalm;
Then our joyful song shall be,
I have overcome through Thee.

FEBRUARY 5.

"Rest in the Lord" (Ps. xxxvii.).

In the old creation the week began with work and ended with Sabbath rest. The resurrection week begins with the first day--first rest, then labor.

So we must first cease from our own works as God did from His, and enter into His rest, and then we will work, with rested hearts, His works with effectual power.

But why "labor to enter into rest"? See that ship--how restfully she sails over the waters, her sails swelling with the gale; and borne without an effort! And yet, look at that man at the helm. See how firmly he holds the rudder, bearing against the wind, and holding her steady to her position. Let him for a moment relax his steady hold and the ship will fall listlessly along the wind. The sails will flap, the waves will toss the vessel at their will, and all rest and power will have gone. It is the fixed helm that brings the steadying power of the wind. And so He has said, "Thou wilt keep him in perfect peace, whose mind is stayed on Thee, because he trusteth in Thee." The steady will and stayed heart are ours. The keeping is the Lord's. So let us labor to enter and abide in His rest.

FEBRUARY 6.

"Praying always for all saints" (Eph. vi. 18).

One good counsel will suffice just now. Stop praying so much for yourself; begin to ask unselfish things, and see if God won't give you faith. See how much easier it will be to believe for another than for your own petty self. Try the effect of praying for the world, for definite things, for difficult things, for glorious things, for things that will honor Christ and save mankind, and after you have received a few wonderful answers to prayer in this direction, see if you won't feel stronger to touch your own little burden with a Divine faith, and then go back again to the high place of unselfish prayer for others.

Have you ever learned the beautiful art of letting God take care of you, and giving all your thought and strength to pray for others and for the kingdom of God? It will relieve you of a thousand cares. It will lift you up into a noble and lofty sphere, and teach you to live and love like God. Lord save us from our selfish prayers and give us the faith that worketh by love, and the heart of Christ for a perishing world.

FEBRUARY 7.

"Faithful in that which is least" (Luke xvi. 10).

The man that missed his opportunity and met the doom of the faithless servant was not the man with five talents, or the man with two, but the man who had only one. The people who are in danger of missing life's great meaning are the people of ordinary capacity and opportunity, and who say to themselves, "There is so little I can do that I will not try to do anything." One of the finest windows in Europe was made from the remnants an apprentice boy collected from the cuttings of his master's great work. The sweepings of the British mint are worth

26

millions. The little pivots on which the works of your watch turn are so important that they are actually made of jewels. And so God places a solemn value and responsibility on the humble workers, the people that try to hide behind their insignificance the trifling opportunities and the single talents; and our littleness will not excuse us in the reckoning day.

"Talk not of talents, what hast thou to do?
Thou hast sufficient, whether five or two.
Talk not of talents; is thy duty done?
This brings the blessing whether ten or one."

FEBRUARY 8.

"We are not sufficient of ourselves to think anything as of ourselves" (II. Cor. iii. 5).

Insufficient, "All sufficient." These two words form the complement of each other and together give the key to an efficient Christian life. The discovery and full conviction of our utter helplessness is the constant condition of spiritual supply. The aim of the Old Testament, therefore, is ever to show man's failure; that of the New, to reveal Christ's sufficiency. He has all things for us, but we cannot receive them till we know that we have nothing.

The very essence, therefore, of Christian perfection is the constant renunciation of our own perfection, and the continual acceptance of Christ's righteousness. And as we receive deeper views of our nothingness and evil, it is but a call to claim more of His rich grace. But it is possible fully to know our insufficiency and yet not take firmly hold of His "all things." This, too, must be done with a faith that will not accept less than ALL. The prophet was angry because the king of Israel had only smitten thrice upon the ground. He should have done it five or six times. He might have had all. So let us meet His greatness and grace.

FEBRUARY 9.

"None of these things move me" (Acts xx. 24).

The best evidence of God's presence is the devil's growl. So wrote good Mr. Spurgeon once in "The Sword and the Trowel," and that little sentence has helped many a tried and tired child Of God to stand fast and even rejoice under the fiercest attacks of the foe.

We read in the book of Samuel that the moment that David was crowned at Hebron, "All the Philistines came up to seek David." And the moment we get anything from the Lord worth contending for, then the devil comes to seek us.

When the enemy meets us at the threshold of any great work for God let us accept it as "a token of salvation," and claim double blessing, victory and power. Power is developed by resistance. The cannon carries twice as far because the exploding power has to find its way through resistance. The way electricity is produced in the power-house yonder is by the sharp friction of the revolving wheels. And so we shall find some day that even Satan has been one of God's agencies of blessing.

FEBRUARY 10.

"I am crucified with Christ; nevertheless I live" (Gal. ii. 20).

Christ life is in harmony with our nature. A lady asked me the other day--a thoughtful, intelligent woman who was not a Christian, but who had the deepest hunger for that which is right: "How can this be so, and we not lose our individuality! This will destroy our personality, and it violates our responsibility as individuals."

I said: "Dear sister, your personality is only half without Christ. Christ was made for you, and you were made for Christ, and until you meet you are not complete, and He needs you as you need Him." I said: "Suppose that gas-jet should say, 'If I take this fire in, the gas will lose its individuality.' Oh, no; it is only when the fire comes in that the gas fulfils its very purpose of being. Suppose the snowflake should say, 'What shall I do? If I drop on the ground I shall lose my individuality.' But it falls and is absorbed by the soil, and the snowflakes are seen by-and-by in the primroses and daisies. Let us lose ourselves and rise to a new life in Christ."

FEBRUARY 11.

"Strengthened with all might unto all patience" (Col. i. 11).

The apostle prays for the Colossians, that they may be "strengthened with all might, according to His glorious power, unto all patience and long-suffering with joyfulness." It is one thing to endure and show the strain on every muscle of your face, and seem to say with every wrinkle, "Why does not somebody sympathize with me?" It is another to endure the cross, "despising the shame" for the joy set before us.

There are some trees in the garden of the Lord which "shall not see when heat cometh"; and shall not be careful in the year of drought, nor cease from yielding fruit. Let us set our faces toward the sunrising and use the clouds that come, to make rainbows. Not much longer shall we have the glorious opportunity to rejoice in tribulation, and learn patience. In heaven we shall have nothing to teach long-suffering. If we do not learn it here, we shall be without our brightest crown forever, and wish ourselves back for a little while, in the very circumstances of which we are now trying so hard to get rid.

FEBRUARY 12.

"But seek ye first the Kingdom of God, and His righteousness, and all these things shall be added unto you" (Matt. vi. 33).

For every heart that is seeking anything from the Lord this is a good watchword. That very thing, or the desire for it, may unconsciously separate you from the Lord, or at least from the singleness of your purpose unto Him. The thing we desire may be a right thing, but we may desire it in a distrusting and selfish spirit. Let us commit it to Him, and not cease to believe for it, but let us, at the same time, keep our purpose fixed on His will and glory, and claim even His promised blessings, not for themselves or ourselves, but for Him. Then shall it be true, "Delight thyself in the Lord, and He shall give thee the desires of thine heart." All other things but Himself God will "_add_." But they must be ever _added_, never _first_.

Then shall we be able to believe for them without doubt, when we claim them for Him and not for ourselves. It is only when "we are Christ's" that "all things are ours."

Lord, help me this day to seek Thee first, and be more desirous to please Thee and have Thy will than to possess any other blessing.

FEBRUARY 13.

"Thy prayers are come up for a memorial before God" (Acts x. 4).

What a beautiful expression the angel used to Cornelius, "Thy prayers are come up for a memorial." It would almost seem as if supplications of years had accumulated before the Throne, and at last the answer broke in blessings on the head of Cornelius, even as the accumulated evaporation of months at last bursts in floods of rain upon the parched ground. So God is represented as treasuring the prayers of His saints in vials; they are described as sweet odors. They are placed like fragrant flowers in the chambers of the King. And kept in sweet remembrance before Him. And later they are represented as poured out upon the earth; and lo, there are voices and thunderings and great providential movements fulfilling God's purposes for His kingdom. We are called "the Lord's remembrancers," and are commanded to give Him no rest, day nor night, but crowd the heavens with our petitions and in due time the answer will come with its accumulated blessings.

No breath of true prayer is lost. The longer it waits, the larger it becomes.

FEBRUARY 14.

"He shall baptize you with fire" (Matt. iii. 11).

Fire is strangely intense and intrinsic. It goes into the very substance of things. It somehow blends with every particle of the thing it touches.

There are the severe trials that come to minds more sensitive, to the minds that have more points of contact with what hurts; so that the higher the nature the higher the joy, and the greater the avenues of pain that come.

And then there are deeper trials that come as we pass into the hands of God, as we pass from the physical and intellectual into the spiritual nature.

When they first come, we shrink back from their unnatural and fearful breath, and we say: "Oh, this cannot be from the hand of a loving Father! This cannot be necessary to me."

And then come the pains and sufferings from God's own hand, when He sits as a refiner and purifier of silver, when He lets it burn, until it seems that we must be burned to ashes, and we are, indeed, at last burned to ashes.

But we must get the victory through faith. The moment you cease to fear it, that moment it ceases to harm you. He says, "The flames shall not kindle upon you."

FEBRUARY 15.

"Be strong in the grace that is in Christ Jesus" (II. Tim. ii. 1).

How to enjoy this day. This will never come by trying to be happy and yet we are responsible for the conditions of real joy.

30

1. Be right with God; for "Gladness is sown for the upright in heart." "It is His joy that remains in us that makes our joy to be full."
2. Forget yourself and live for others; for "It is more blessed to give than to receive."
3. When you cannot rejoice in feelings, circumstances and states, "rejoice in the Lord," and "count it all joy, when ye fall into divers temptations."

Finally, obey the Lord and be faithful to your trust; and again and again will His blessed Spirit whisper to your heart, "Well done, good and faithful servant, enter into the joy of thy Lord."

"Not enjoyment and not sorrow

Is our destined end or way,

But to act that each to-morrow

Finds us farther than to-day.

"Let us then be up and doing

With a heart for any fate,

Still achieving, still pursuing,

Learn to labor and to wait."

FEBRUARY 16.

"We will give ourselves continually to prayer" (Acts vi. 4).

In the consecrated believer the Holy Spirit is pre-eminently a Spirit of prayer. If our whole being is committed to Him, and our thoughts are at His bidding, He will occupy every moment in communion and we shall bring every thing to Him as it comes, and pray it out in our spiritual consciousness before we act it out in our lives. We shall, therefore, find ourselves taking up the burdens of life and praying them out in a wordless prayer which we ourselves often cannot understand, but which is simply the unfolding of His thought and will within us, and which will be followed by the unfolding of His providence concerning us.

Want of faithfulness and obedience to the faintest whisper of His will will often hinder some blessing which He meant for us until after a while we may get so dull and negligent that He will not be able to trust us with His whispers and we shall thus stumble on in the darkness and miss His highest thoughts.

Lord, teach us to pray in the Spirit, to pray without ceasing and to lose nothing of Thy will.

FEBRUARY 17.

"Your life is hid" (Col. iii. 3).

Some Christians loom up in larger proportion than is becoming. They can tell, and others can tell, how many souls they bring to Christ. Their labor seems to crystallize and become its own memorial. Others again seem to blend so wholly with other workers that their own individuality can scarcely be traced. And yet, after all, this is the most Christ-like ministry of all, for the Master Himself does not even appear in the work of the church except as her hidden Life and ascended Head, and even the Holy Spirit is lost in the vessels that He uses. The vine does not bear the fruit, and even the sap is unseen in its ceaseless flow, and it is the little branches which bear all the clusters and seem to have all the honor of the vintage. And so the nearer we come to Christ the more we are willing to be lost sight of in our fruit, and let others be more prominent, while we are the glad and willing witnesses of our testimony and hold up their hands by the silent ministry of love and prayer. Lord, let me be like the veiled seraphim before the throne, who cover their faces and their feet, and hide themselves and their service while they fly to obey Thee.

FEBRUARY 18.

"Christ in you" (Col. i. 27).

How great the difference between the old and the new way of deliverance! One touch of Christ is worth a lifetime of struggling. A sufferer in one of our hospitals was in danger of losing his sight from a small piece of broken needle that had entered his eye.

Operation after operation had only irritated it, and driven the foreign substance farther still into the delicate nerves of the sensitive organ. At length a skilful young physician thought of a new expedient. He came one day without lancet and probes, and holding in his hand a small but powerful magnet, which he kept before the wounded eye, as close as it could bear. Immediately the piece of steel began to move toward the powerful attraction, and soon flew up to meet it and left the suffering eye completely relieved, without an effort or a laceration. It was as simple as it was wonderful. By a single touch of power the organ was saved and a dangerous trouble completely cured.

It is thus that God delivers us, by the simple attraction of Christ's life and power.

FEBRUARY 19.

32

"As much as in me is I am ready" (Rom. i. 15).

Be earnest. Intense earnestness, a whole heart for Christ, the passion sign of the cross, the enthusiasm of our whole being for our Master and humanity--this is what the Lord expects, this is what His cross deserves, this is what the world needs, this is what the age has a right to look for. Everything around us is intensely alive. Life is earnest, death is earnest, sin is earnest, men are earnest, business is earnest, knowledge is earnest, the age is earnest; God forgive us if we alone are trifling in the white heat of this crisis time. Oh, for the baptism of fire! Oh, for the living coal upon the burning lips of love! Oh, for men God-possessed and self-surrendered grasping God's great idea and pressing forward "for the mark of the prize of the high calling of God in Christ Jesus."

All the world for Jesus

My prayer shall be,

And my watchword ever,

Himself for me.

All the world for Jesus,

Lord, quickly come,

Bring Thy promised kingdom,

And take us home.

FEBRUARY 20.

"Fear thou not, for I am with thee" (Isa. xli. 10).

Satan is always trying to weaken our faith by fear. He is a great metaphysician and knows the paralyzing effect of fear, that it is the great enemy of faith, and that faith is the great secret of help. If he can get us fearing he will stop our trusting and hinder the very blessing we need. Job found the peril of fear and gives us the sorrowful testimony, "I feared a fear and it came upon me."

Fear is born of Satan, and if we would only take time to think a moment we would see that everything Satan says is founded upon a falsehood. He is the father of lies. Even his fears are falsehoods and his terrors ought rather be to us encouragements.

When Satan tells you, therefore, that some ill is going to come, you may quietly look in his face and tell him he is a liar, that instead of ill, goodness and mercy shall follow you all the days of your life, and then turn to your blessed

33

Lord and say, "What time I am afraid, I will trust in Thee." Every fear is distrust and trust is the remedy for fear. "What time I am afraid I will _trust_ in thee."

FEBRUARY 21.

"Be not dismayed, for I am thy God" (Isa. xli. 10).

How tenderly God is always comforting our fears! How sweetly He says in Isaiah xli. 10, "Fear not; for I am with thee: be not dismayed; for I am thy God: I will uphold thee with the right hand of My righteousness." And yet again with still tenderer thoughtfulness, "I, the Lord thy God, will hold thy right hand, saying unto thee, Fear not, I will help thee." Not only does He say it once, but He keeps holding our right hand and repeating such promises.

The blessed Lord has condensed it all into one sweet monogram of eternal comfort in His message to the disciples on the sea of Galilee, "It is I; be not afraid." He does not say, "It is over," or "It is morning," or "It is fine weather," or "It is smooth water," but He says, "It is I, be not afraid." He is the antidote to fear; He is the remedy for trouble; He is the substance and the sum of deliverance. Therefore, we should rise above fear. Let us keep our eyes fastened upon Him; let us abide continually in Him; let us be content with Him; let us cling closely to Him and cry, "We will not fear though the earth be removed, though the mountains be carried into the midst of the sea."

FEBRUARY 22.

"He that hath entered into His rest hath ceased from his own works even as God did from His" (Heb. iv. 10).

What a rest it would be to many of us if we could but exchange burdens with Christ, and so utterly and forever transfer to Him all our cares and needs that we would not feel henceforth responsible for our burdens, but know that He has undertaken all the care, and that our faith is simply to carry His burdens, and that He prays, labors, and suffers only for us and our interests. This is what He truly invites us to do. "Come unto Me," He says, "all ye that labor and are heavy-laden and I will rest you," and then He adds, "Take My yoke upon you, and learn of Me." He takes our yoke and we take His and we find it a thousand times easier to carry one of His burdens than to carry our own. How much more delightful it is to spend an hour in supplication for another than five minutes in pleading for ourselves. Are we not weary of carrying our wretched loads?

'Twas for this His mercy sought you,

And to all His fulness brought you,

By the precious blood that bought you,

Pass it on.

FEBRUARY 23.

"For me to live is Christ and to die is gain" (Phil. i. 21).

The secret of a sound body is a sound heart, and the prayer of the Holy Ghost for us is, that we "may be in health and prosper even as our soul prospers."

We find Paul in the Epistles to the Philippians expressing a sublime and holy indifference to the question of life or death. Indeed he is in a real strait, whether he would prefer "to depart and be with Christ," or to remain still in the flesh.

The former would indeed be his sweetest preference, but the latter would be at the same time a joyful service. His only object in wanting to live is to be a blessing. "To abide in the flesh is more needful to you."

Having reached this state of heart, it is beautiful to notice how quickly he rises to the victorious faith necessary to claim perfect strength and health. Because it is more needful to you that I abide in the flesh, he adds, "I know that I shall continue with you all, for your furtherance and joy of faith." Lord, help me to-day to "count not my life dear unto myself that I may finish my course with joy and the ministry that I have received of Jesus."

FEBRUARY 24.

"Sin shall not have dominion over you, for ye are not under the law, but under grace" (Rom. vi. 14).

The secret of Moses' failures was this: "The law made nothing perfect, but the bringing in of a better hope did." And this was why his life work also came short of full realization. He saw but entered not the Promised Land. The founder of the law had to be its victim, and his life and death might demonstrate the inability of the law to lead any man into the Promised Land. The very fact, that it was for so slight a fault that Moses lost his inheritance, makes all the more emphatic the solemn sentence of the law. "Cursed is every one that continueth not in all things that are written in the Book of the Law to do them."

But to the glory of the grace of God we can add that what the law could not do for Moses the Gospel did; and he who could not pass over the Jordan under the old dispensation is seen on the very heights of Hermon with the Son of Man, sharing His Transfiguration glory, and talking of that death on Calvary to which be owed his glorious destiny.

That grace we have inherited under the Gospel of Jesus Christ.

FEBRUARY 25.

"I am the vine, ye are the branches" (John xv. 5).

How can I take Christ as my Sanctifier, or Healer? is a question that we are constantly asked. It is necessary first of all that we get into the posture of faith. This has to be done by a definite and voluntary act, and then maintained by a uniform habit. It is just the same as the planting of a tree. You must put it in the soil by a definite act, and then you must let it stay put and remain settled in the ground until the little roots have time to fix themselves and begin to draw the sustenance from the soil. There are two stages, the definite planting and then the habitual absorbing of moisture and nourishment from the ground. The root fibers must rest until they reach out their spongy pores and drink in the nutriment of the earth. After the habit is established, then by a certain uniform law, the plant draws its life from the ground without an effort, and it is just as natural for it to grow as it is for us to breathe.

Lord, help me this day to abide in Thee, and to grow into the habit of drawing all my life from Thine so that it shall be true for me, "In Him I live and move and have my being."

FEBRUARY 26.

"Make you perfect in every good work" (Heb. xiii. 21).

In that beautiful prayer at the close of the Epistle to the Hebrews, "Now the God of peace, that brought again from the dead, our Lord Jesus Christ, that great Shepherd of the sheep, through the blood of the everlasting covenant, make you perfect in every good work to do His will," the phrase, "make you perfect in every good work," literally means, it is said, "adjust you in every good work." It is a great thing to be adjusted, adjusted to our surroundings and circumstances rather than trying to have them adjusted to us, adjusted to the people we are thrown with, adjusted to the work God has for us, and not trying to get God to help us to do our work; adjusted to do the very will and plan of God for us in our whole life. This is the secret of rest, power and freedom in our life-work.

36

"Oh, fill me with Thy fulness, Lord.

Until my very heart o'erflow

In kindling thought and glowing word,

Thy love to tell, Thy praise to show.

Oh, use me, Lord, use even me,

Just as Thou wilt, and when, and where;

Until Thy blessed face I see,

Thy rest, Thy joy, Thy glory share."

FEBRUARY 27.

"Stablish, strengthen, settle you" (I. Peter v. 10).

In taking Christ in any new relationship, we must first have sufficient intellectual light to satisfy our mind that we are entitled to stand in this relationship. The shadow of a question here will wreck our confidence. Then, having seen this, we must make the venture, the committal, the choice, and take the place just as definitely as the tree is planted in the soil, or the bride gives herself away at the marriage altar. It must be once for all, without reserve, without recall.

Then there is a season of establishing, settling and testing, during which we must stay put until the new relationship gets so fixed as to become a permanent habit. It is just the same as when the surgeon sets the broken arm. He puts it in splints to keep it from vibration. So God has His spiritual splints that He wants to put upon His children and keep them quiet and unmoved until they pass the first stage of faith.

It is not always easy work for us, "but the God of all grace who hath called you unto His eternal glory by Christ Jesus after you have suffered awhile, stablish, strengthen, settle you."

FEBRUARY 28.

"Count it all joy" (James i. 2).

We do not always feel joyful, but we are to count it all joy. The word "reckon" is one of the key-words of Scripture. It is the same word used about our being dead. We do not feel dead. We are painfully conscious of something that would gladly return to life. But we are to treat ourselves as dead, and neither fear nor obey the old nature.

So we are to reckon the thing that comes as a blessing. We are determined to rejoice, to say, "My heart is fixed, O God, I will sing and give praise." This rejoicing, by faith, will soon become a habit, and will ever bring speedily the spirit of gladness and the spontaneous overflow of praise.

Then, "although the fig-tree may wither and no fruit appear in the vines, the labor of the olive fail and the fields yield no increase, the herd be cut off from the stall, and the cattle from the field, yet we will rejoice in the Lord, and joy in the God of our salvation."

"Peace, perfect peace, with sorrows surging round,

On Jesus' bosom naught but calm is found;

Peace, perfect peace, our future all unknown,

Jesus we know, and He is on the throne."

MARCH 1.

"Wait on the Lord" (Ps. xxvii. 14).

How often this is said in the Bible, how little understood! It is what the old monk calls the "practice of the presence of God." It is the habit of prayer. It is the continued communion that not only asks, but receives. People often ask us to pray for them and we have to say, "Why, God has answered our prayer for you, and you must now take the answer. It is awaiting you, and you must take it by waiting on the Lord."

This it is that renews the strength, until we mount up with wings as eagles, run and are not weary, walk and are not faint. Our hearts are too vast to take in His fulness at a single breath. We must live in the atmosphere of His presence till we absorb His very life. This is the secret of spiritual depth and rest, of power and fulness, of love and prayer, of hope and holy usefulness. "Wait, I say, on the Lord."

I am waiting in communion at the blessed mercy seat,

I am waiting, sweetly waiting, on the Lord;

I am drinking, of His fulness; I am sitting at His feet;

I am hearkening to the whispers of His word.

MARCH 2.

"That good thing which was committed unto thee keep by the Holy Ghost" (II. Tim. i. 14).

38

God gives to us a power within which will hold our hearts in victory and purity. "That good thing which was committed unto thee, keep by the Holy Ghost which dwelleth in us." It is the Holy Ghost; and when any thought or suggestion of evil arises in our breast, the quick conscience can instantly call upon the Holy Ghost to drive it out, and He will expel it at the command of faith or prayer, and keep us as pure as we are willing to be kept. But when the will surrenders and consents to evil, the Holy Ghost will not expel it. God, then, requires us to stand in holy vigilance, and He will do exceeding abundantly for us as we hold fast that which is good, and He will also be in us a spirit of vigilance, showing us the evil and enabling us to detect it, and to bring it to Him for expulsion and destruction.

"O Spirit of Jesus fill us until we shall have room only for Thee!"

O, come as the heart-searching fire,

O, come as the sin-cleansing flood;

Consume us with holy desire,

And fill with the fulness of God.

MARCH 3.

"Now no chastening for the present seemeth to be joyous but grievous; nevertheless afterward" (Heb. xii. 11).

God seems to love to work by paradoxes and contraries. In the transformations of grace, the bitter is the base of the sweet, night is the mother of day, and death is the gate of life.

Many people are wanting power. Now, how is power produced? The other day we passed the great works where the trolley engines are supplied with electricity. We heard the hum and roar of countless wheels, and we asked our friend, "How do they make the power?" "Why," he said, "just by the revolution of those wheels and the friction they produce. The rubbing creates the electric current."

It is very simple, and a trifling experiment will prove it to any one.

And so when God wants to bring more power into your life, He brings more pressure. He is generating spiritual force by hard rubbing. Some of us don't like it. Some of us don't understand, and we try to run away from the pressure, instead of getting the power and using it to rise above the painful cause.

MARCH 4.

"They were all filled with the Holy Ghost" (Acts ii. 4).

Blessed secret of spiritual purity, victory and joy, of physical life and healing, and all power for service. Filled with the Spirit there is no room for self or sin, for fret or care. Filled with the Spirit we repel the elements of disease that are in the air as the red-hot iron repels the water that touches it. Filled with the Spirit we are always ready for service, and Satan turns away when he finds the Holy Ghost enrobing us in His garments of holy flame. Not half-filled, but filled with the Spirit is the place of victory and power.

This is not only a privilege; it is a command, and He who gave it will enable us to fulfill it if we bring it to Him with an empty, honest, trusting heart, and claim our privilege in the name of Jesus and for the glory of God.

Holy Ghost, I bid Thee welcome;

Come and be my Holy Guest;

Heavenly Dove within my bosom,

Make Thy home and build Thy nest;

Lead me on to all Thy fulness,

Bring me to Thy Promised Rest,

Holy Ghost, I bid Thee welcome,

Come and be my Holy Guest.

MARCH 5.

"I have overcome the world" (John xvi. 33).

Christ has overcome for us every one of our four terrible foes--Sin, Sickness, Sorrow, Satan. He has borne our Sin, and we may lay all, even down to our sinfulness itself, on Him. "I have overcome for thee." He has borne our sickness, and we may detach ourselves from our old infirmities and rise into His glorious life and strength. He has borne our sorrows, and we must not even carry a care, but rejoice evermore, and even glory in tribulations also. And He has conquered Satan for us, too, and left him nailed to the cross, spoiled and dishonored and but a shadow of himself. And now we have but to claim His full atonement and assert our victory, and so "overcome him by the blood of the Lamb and the word of our testimony."

Beloved, are we overcoming sin? Are we overcoming sickness? Are we overcoming sorrow? Are we overcoming Satan?

40

Fear not, though the strife be long;
Faint not, though the foe be strong;
Trust thy glorious Captain's power;
Watch with Him one little hour,
Hear Him calling, "Follow me.
"I have overcome for thee."

MARCH 6.

"Lean not unto thine own understanding" (Prov. iii. 5).

Faith is hindered by reliance upon human wisdom, whether our own or the wisdom of others. The devil's first bait to Eve was an offer of wisdom, and for this she sold her faith. "Ye shall be as gods," he said, "knowing good and evil," and from the hour she began to know she ceased to trust. It was the spies that lost the Land of Promise to Israel of old. It was their foolish proposition to search out the land, and find out by investigation whether God had told the truth or not, that led to the awful outbreak of unbelief that shut the doors of Canaan to a whole generation. It is very significant that the names of these spies are nearly all suggestive of human wisdom, greatness and fame.

So in the days of Christ, it was the bondage of the Jews to the traditions of their fathers and the opinions of men, that kept them back from receiving Him. "How can ye believe," He asked, "which receive honor from men, and seek not that which cometh from God only?"

Let us trust Him with all our heart and lean not to our own understanding.

MARCH 7.

"It is more blessed to give than to receive" (Acts xx. 35).

How shall we know the difference between the earthly and the heavenly love? The one terminates on ourselves and is partly ourself seeking its own gratification. The other reaches out to God and others, and finds its joy in glorifying Him and blessing them. Love is unselfishness, and the love that is not unselfish is not divine. How much do we pray for others, and how much for ourselves? What is the center of our being? Ourselves, or our Lord and His people and work? The Lord help us to know more fully the meaning of that great truth, "It is more blessed to give than to receive." "He that saveth his life shall lose it, and he that loseth his life for My sake and the Gospel, shall keep it unto life eternal."

Have you found some precious treasure,

Pass it on.

Have You found some holy pleasure,

Pass it on.

Giving out is twice possessing,

Love will double every blessing,

On to higher service pressing,

Pass it on.

MARCH 8.

"Pray Ye therefore" (Luke x. 2).

Prayer is the mighty engine that is to move the missionary work. "Pray ye therefore the Lord of the harvest that He will send forth laborers into His harvest."

We are asking God to touch the hearts of men every day by the Holy Ghost, so that they shall be compelled to go abroad and preach the Gospel. We are asking Him to wake them up at night with the solemn conviction that the heathen are perishing, and that their blood will be upon their souls, and God is answering the prayer by sending persons to us every day who "feel that the King's business requireth haste."

Beloved, pray, pray, pray; and as the incense rises to the heavens, "there will be silence in heaven" by the space of more than half an hour, and the coals of fire will be emptied out upon the earth, and the coming of the Lord will begin to draw nearer. Pray till the Lord of the harvest shall thrust forth laborers into His harvest.

Send the coals of heavenly fire,

From the altar of the skies;

Fill our hearts with strong desire,

Till our pray'rs like incense rise.

MARCH 9.

"How ye ought to walk and please God" (I. Thess. iv. 1).

How many dear Christians are in the place that the Lord has appointed them, and yet the devil is harassing their lives with a vague sense of not quite pleasing

42

the Lord. Could they just settle down in the place that God has assigned them and fill it sweetly and lovingly for Him there would be more joy in their hearts and more power in their lives. God wants us all in various places, and the secret of accomplishing the most for Him is to recognize our places from Him and our service in it as pleasing Him. In the great factory and machine there is a place for the smallest screw and rivet as well as the great driving wheel and piston, and so God has His little screws whose business is simply to stay where He puts them and to believe that He wants them there and is making the most of their lives in the little spaces that they fill for Him.

There is something all can do,

Tho' you're neither wise nor strong;

You can be a helper true,

You can stand when friends are few,

Some lone heart has need of you,

You can help along.

MARCH 10.

"The peace of God which passeth all understanding shall keep your hearts and minds" (Phil. iv. 7).

It is not peace with God, but the peace of God. "The peace that passes all understanding" is the very breath of God in the soul. He alone is able to keep it, and He can so keep it that "nothing shall offend us." Beloved, are you there?

God's rest did not come till after His work was over, and ours will not. We begin our Christian life by working, trying and struggling in the energy of the flesh to save ourselves. At last, when we are able to cease from our own work, God comes in with His blessed rest, and works His own Divine works in us.

Oh! have you heard the glorious word

Of hope and holy cheer;

From heav'n above its tones of love

Are lingering on my ear;

The blessed Comforter has come,

And Christ will soon be here.

Oh, hearts that sigh there's succor nigh,

The Comforter is near;

He comes to bring us to our King,

And fit us to appear.

I'm glad the Comforter has come,

And Christ will soon be here.

MARCH 11.

"But ye are a chosen generation, a peculiar people" (I. Peter ii. 9).

We have been thinking lately very much of the strange way in which God is calling a people out of a people already called. The word _ecclesia_, or church, means called out, but God is calling out a still more select body from the church to be His bride--the specially prepared ones for His coming.

We see a fine type of this in the story of Gideon. When first he sounded the trumpet of Abiezer there resorted to him more than thirty thousand men; but these had to be picked, so a first test was applied, appealing to their courage, and all but ten thousand went back; but there must be an election out of the election, and so a second test was applied, appealing to their prudence, caution and singleness of purpose, and all but three hundred were refused; and, with this little picked band, he raised the standard against the Midianites, and through the power of God won his glorious victory. So, again, in our days, the Master is choosing His three hundred, and by them He will yet win the world for Himself. Let us be sure that we belong to the "out and out" people.

MARCH 12.

"They wandered in the wilderness in a solitary way" (Ps. cvii. 4).

All who fight the Lord's battles must be content to die to all the favorable opinions of men and all the flattery of human praise. You cannot make an exception in favor of the good opinions of the children of God. It is very easy for the insidious adversary to make this also all appeal to the flesh. It is all right when God sends us the approval of our fellow men, but we must never make it a motive in our life, but be content with the "solitary way" and the lonely "wilderness."

All such motives are poison and a taking away from you of the strength with which you are to give glory to God. It is not the fact that all that see the face of the Lord do see each other.

The man of God must walk alone with God. He must be contented that the Lord knoweth that God knows. It is such a relief to the natural man within us to fall back upon human countenances and human thoughts and sympathy, that we often deceive ourselves and think it "brotherly love," when we are just resting in the earthly sympathy of some fellow worm!

MARCH 13.

"Keep yourselves in the love of God" (Jude 21).

Some time ago, we were enjoying a surpassingly beautiful sunset. The western skies seemed like a great archipelago of golden islands, the masses in the distance rising up into vast mountains of glory. The hue of the sky was so gorgeous that it seemed to reflect itself upon the whole atmosphere, as we looked back from the west to the eastern horizon. The whole earth was radiant with glory. The fields had changed to strange, red richness, and the earth seemed bathed with the dews of heaven.

And so it is, when the love of God shines through all our celestial sky, it covers everything below, and life becomes radiant with its light. Things that were hard become easy. Things that were sharp become sweet. Labor loses its burden, and sorrow becomes silver-lined with hope and gladness.

There are two ways of living in His love. One is constant trust, and the other is constant obedience, and His own Word gives the message for both. "If ye keep My commandments ye shall live in My love, even as I keep My Father's, and live in His love."

MARCH 14.

"We are His workmanship" (Eph. ii. 10).

Christ sends us to serve Him, not in our own strength, but in His resources and might. "We are His workmanship, created in Christ Jesus unto good works, which God hath prepared that we should walk in them." We do not have to prepare them; but to wear them as garments, made to order for every occasion of our life.

We must receive them by faith and go forth in His work, believing that He is with us, and in us, as our all sufficiency for wisdom, faith, love, prayer, power, and every grace and gift that our work requires. In this work of faith we shall have to feel weak and helpless, and even have little consciousness of power. But if we believe and go forward, He will be the power and send the fruits.

The most useful services we render are those which, like the sweet fruits of the wilderness, spring from hours of barrenness. "I will bring her into the wilderness and I will give her vineyards from thence." Let us learn to work by faith as well as walk by faith, then we shall receive even the end of our faith, the salvation of precious souls, and our lives will bear fruit which shall be manifest throughout all eternity.

MARCH 15.

"Continue ye in My love" (John xv. 9).

Many atmospheres there are in which we may live. Some people live in an atmosphere of thought. Their faces are thoughtful, minds intellectual. They live in their ideas, their conceptions of truth, their tastes, and esthetic nature. Some people, again, live in their animal nature, in the lusts of the flesh and eye, the coarse, low atmosphere of a sensuous life, or something worse. Some, again, live in a world of duty. The predominating feature of their life is conscience, and it carries with it a certain shadowy fear that takes away the simple freedom and gladness of life, but there is a rectitude, and uprightness, a strictness of purpose, and of conduct which cannot be gainsaid or questioned.

But Christ bids us live in an atmosphere of love. "As My Father has loved Me, so have I loved you; continue ye in My love." In the original it is, "Live in My love." Love is the atmosphere that He would have us ever live in, that is, believing that He ever loves us, and claiming His sweet approval and tender regard. This is a life of love.

MARCH 16.

"The Lord will give grace and glory" (Ps. lxxxiv. 11).

The Lord will give grace and glory. This word _glory_ is very difficult to translate, define and explain; but there is something in the spiritual consciousness of the quickened Christian that interprets it. It is the overflow of grace; it is the wine of life; it is the foretaste of heaven; it is a flash from the Throne and an inspiration from the heart of God which we may have and in which we may live. "The glory which Thou hast given Me I have given them," the Master prayed for us. Let us take it and live in it. David used to say, "Wake up my glory." Ask God to wake up your glory and enable you to mount up with wings as eagles, to dwell on high and sit with Christ in the heavenly places.

Mounting up with wings as eagles,
Waiting on the Lord we rise,
Strength exchanging, life renewing,
How our spirit heavenward flies.
Then our springing feet returning,
Tread the pathway of the saint,
We shall run and not be weary,
We shall walk and never faint.

MARCH 17.

"He hath remembered His covenant forever" (Ps. cv. 8).

So long as you struggle under law, that is by your own effort, sin shall have dominion over you: but the moment you step from under the shadow of Sinai, throw yourself upon the simple grace of Christ and His free and absolute gift of righteousness, and take Him to be to you what He has pledged Himself to be, your righteousness of thought and feeling, and to keep you in spite of everything, that ever can be against you, in His perfect will and peace, the struggle is practically over. Beloved, do you really know and believe that this is the very promise of the Gospel, the very essence of the new covenant, that Christ pledges Himself to put His law in your heart, and to cause you to walk in His statutes, and to keep His judgments and do them? Do you know that this is the oath which He sware unto Abraham, that He would grant unto us. "That we being delivered from the hands of our enemies, and from all that hate us, might serve Him without fear, in righteousness and holiness before Him all the days of our life." He has sworn to do this for you, and He is faithful, that promised. Trust Him ever.

MARCH 18.

"Neither shall any plague come near thy dwelling" (Ps. xci. 10).

We know what it is to be fireproof, to be waterproof: but it is a greater thing to be proof against sin. It is possible to be so filled with the Spirit and presence of Jesus that all the shafts of the enemy glance off our heavenly armor; that all the burrs and thistles which grow on the wayside fail to stick to our heavenly robes;

47

that all the noxious vapors of the pit disappear before the warm breath of the Holy Ghost, and we walk with a charmed life even through the valley of the shadow of death. The red hot iron repels the water that touches it, and the fingers that would trifle with it: and, if we are on fire with the Holy Ghost, Satan will keep his fingers off us, and the cold water that he pours over us will roll off and leave us unharmed: "for He that was begotten of God keepeth us, and that wicked one toucheth us not."

It is said that before going into a malarious region, it is well to fortify the system with nourishing food. So we should be fed and filled by the life of Christ in such a way that the evil does not really touch our life.

MARCH 19.

"Launch out into the deep" (Luke v. 4).

Many difficulties and perplexities in connection with our Christian life might be best settled by a simple and bold decision of our will to go forward with the light we have and leave the speculations and theories that we cannot decide for further settlement. What we need is to act, and to act with the best light we have, and as we step out into the present duty and full obedience, many things will be made plain which it is no use waiting to decide.

Beloved, cut the Gordian knot, like Alexander, with the sword of decision. Launch out into the deep with a bold plunge, and Christ will settle for you all the questions that you are now debating, and more probably show you their insignificance, and let you see that the only way to settle them is to overleap them. They are Satan's petty snares to waste your time and keep you halting when you should be marching on.

The mercy of God is an ocean divine,

A boundless and fathomless flood;

Launch out in the deep, cut away the shore line,

And be lost in the fulness of God.

MARCH 20.

"They which receive abundance of grace and the gift of righteousness shall reign in life" (Rom. v. 17).

Precious souls sometimes fight tremendous battles in order to attain to righteousness in trying places. Perhaps the heart has become wrong in some

48

matter where temptation has been allowed to overcome, or at least to turn it aside from its singleness unto God; and the conflict is a terrible one as it seeks to adjust itself and be right with God, and finds itself baffled by its own spiritual foes, and its own helplessness, perplexity and perversity. How dark and dreary the struggle, and how helpless and ineffectual it often seems at such times! It is almost sure to strive in the spirit of the law, and the result always is, and must ever be, condemnation and failure. Every disobedience is met by a blow of wrath, and discouragement, and it well nigh sinks to despair. Oh, if the tempted and struggling one could only understand or remember what perhaps he has learned before, that Christ is our righteousness, and that it is not by law but by grace alone, "For sin shall not have dominion over you, for ye are not under the law, but under grace." That is the secret of the whole battle.

MARCH 21.

"Casting all your care upon Him" (I. Peter v. 7).

Some things there are that God will not tolerate in us. We must leave them. Nehemiah would not talk with Sanballat about his charges and fears, but simply refused to have anything to do with the matter--even to go into the temple and pray about it. How very few things we really have to do with in life. If we would only drop all the needless things and simply do the things that absolutely touch and require our attention from morning till night, we would find what a small slender thread life was; but we string upon it a thousand imaginary beads that never come, and burden ourselves with cares and flurries that if we had trusted more, would never have needed to preoccupy our attention. Wise indeed was the testimony of the dear old saint who said, in review of her past life, "I have had a great many troubles in my life, especially those that never came."

Trust and rest with heart abiding,
Like a birdling in its nest,
Underneath His feathers hiding,
Fold thy wings and trust and rest.
Trust and rest, trust and rest,
God is working for the best.

MARCH 22.

"Hold fast the confidence and the rejoicing of the hope firm unto the end" (Heb. iii. 6).

The attitude of faith is simple trust. It is Elijah saying to Ahab, "There is a sound of abundance of rain." But then there comes usually a deeper experience in which the prayer is inwrought; it is Elijah on the mount, with his face between his knees, travailing, as it were, in birth for the promised blessing. He has believed for it--and now he must take. The first is Joash shooting the arrow out of the windows, but the second is Joash smiting on the ground and following up his faith by perseverance and victorious testing.

It is in this latter place that many of us come short. We ask much from God, and when God proceeds to give it to us we are not found equal to His expectation. We are made partakers of Christ if we hold the beginning of our confidence steadfast to the end, and trust Him through it all.

Fainting soldier of the Lord,

Hear His sweet inspiring word,

"I have conquered all thy foes.

I have suffered all thy woes;

Struggling soldier, trust in Me,

I have overcome for thee."

MARCH 23.

"He is a new creature" (II. Cor. v. 17).

Resurrected, not raised. There is so much in this distinction. The teaching of human philosophy is that we are to raise humanity to a higher plane. This is not the Gospel. On the contrary, the teaching of the cross is that humanity must die and sink out of sight and then be resurrected, not raised. Resurrection is not improvement. It is not elevation, but it is a new supernatural life lifting us from nothingness into God and making us partakers of the Divine nature. It is a new creation. It is an infinite elevation above the highest plane. Let us not take less than resurrection life.

I am crucified with Jesus,

And the cross has set me free;

I have ris'n again with Jesus,

And He lives and reigns in me.

50

This the story of the Master,

Through the cross He reached the throne,

And like Him our path to glory,

Ever leads through death alone.

Lord, teach me the death-born life. Lord, let me live in the power of Thy resurrection!

MARCH 24.

"And again I say, rejoice" (Phil. iv. 4).

It is a good thing to rejoice in the Lord. Perhaps you found the first dose ineffectual. Keep on with your medicine, and when you cannot feel any joy, when there is no spring, and no seeming comfort and encouragement, still rejoice, and count it all joy. Even when you fall into divers temptations, reckon it joy, and delight, and God will make your reckoning good. Do you suppose your Father will let you carry the banner of His victory and His gladness on to the front of the battle, and then coolly stand back and see you captured or beaten back by the enemy? Never! the Holy Spirit will sustain you in your bold advance, and fill your heart with gladness and praise, and you will find your heart all exhilarated and refreshed by the fulness of the heart within.

Lord, teach me to rejoice in Thee, and to rejoice evermore.

The joy of the Lord is the strength of His people.

The sunshine that scatters their sadness and gloom;

The fountain that bursts in the desert of sorrow,

And sheds o'er the wilderness, gladness and bloom.

MARCH 25.

"The beauty of holiness" (Ps. xxix. 2).

Some one remarked once that he did not know more disagreeable people than sanctified Christians. He probably meant people that only profess sanctification. There is an angular, hard, unlovely type of Christian character that is not true holiness; at least, not the highest type of it. It is the skeleton without the flesh covering; it is the naked rock without the vines and foliage that cushion its rugged sides. Jesus was not only virtuous and pure, but He was also beautiful and full of the sweet attractiveness of love.

We read of two kinds of graces: First, "Whatsoever things are just, whatsoever things are lovely and of good report." There are a thousand little graces in Christian life that we cannot afford to ignore. In fact, the last stages in any work of art are always the finishing touches; and so let us not wonder if God shall spend a great deal of time in teaching us the little things that many might consider trifles.

God would have His Bride without a spot or even a wrinkle.

MARCH 26.

"Jesus, the author and finisher of our faith" (Heb. xii. 2).

Add to your faith--do not add to yourself. This is where we make the mistake. We must not only enter by faith, but we must advance by faith each step of the way. At every new stage we shall find ourselves as incompetent and unequal for the pressure as before, and we must take the grace and the victory simply by faith. Is it courage? We shall find ourselves lacking in the needed courage; we must claim it by faith. Is it love? Our own love will be inadequate; but we must take His love, and we shall find it given. Is it faith itself? We must have the faith of God, and Christ in us will be the spirit of faith, as well as the blessing that faith claims. So our whole life from beginning to end, is but Christ in us--in the exceeding riches of His grace; and our everlasting song will be: Not I; but Christ who liveth in me.

'Tis so sweet to walk with Jesus,

Step by step and day by day;

Stepping in His very footprints,

Walking with Him all the way.

MARCH 27.

"What time I am afraid, I will trust in Thee" (Ps. lvi. 3).

We shall never forget a remark Mr. George Mueller once made in answer to a gentleman who asked him the best way to have strong faith. "The only way," replied the patriarch of faith, "to learn strong faith is to endure great trials. I have learned my faith by standing firm amid severe testings." This is very true. The time to trust is when all else fails. Dear one, if you scarcely realize the value of your present opportunity, if you are passing through great afflictions, you are in the very soul of the strongest faith, and if you will only let go, He will teach you in these hours the mightiest hold upon this throne which you can ever know. "Be not afraid, only believe"; and if you are afraid, just look up and say, "What time I am afraid, I will trust in Thee," and you will yet thank God for the school of sorrow which was to you the school of faith.

O brother, give heed to the warning,
And obey His voice to-day.
The Spirit to thee is calling,
O do not grieve Him away.

MARCH 28.

"The fruit of the Spirit is all goodness" (Gal. v. 22).

Goodness is a fruit of the Spirit. Goodness is just "Godness." It is to be like God. And God-like goodness has special reference to the active benevolence of God. The apostle gives us the difference between goodness and righteousness in this passage in Romans, "Scarcely for a righteous man would one die, yet peradventure for a good man some would even dare to die." The righteous man is the man of stiff, inflexible uprightness; but he may be as hard as a granite mountain side. The good man is that mountain side all covered with velvet moss and flowers, and flowing with cascades and springs. Goodness respects "whatsoever things are lovely." It is kindness, affectionateness, benevolence, sympathy, rejoicing with them that do rejoice, and weeping with them that weep. Lord, fill us with Thyself, and let us be God-men and good men, and so represent Thy goodness.

There are lonely hearts to cherish,
While the days are going by;
There are weary souls who perish,
While the days are going by.

MARCH 29.

"He will keep the feet of His saints" (I. Sam. ii. 9).

Perils as well as privileges attend the higher Christian life. The nearer we come to God, the thicker the hosts of darkness in heavenly places. The safe place lies in obedience to God's Word, singleness of heart, and holy vigilance.

When Christians speak of standing in a place where they do not need to watch, they are in great danger. Let us walk in sweet and holy confidence, and yet with

53

holy, humble watchfulness, and "He will keep the feet of His saints." And "now unto Him who is able to keep us from stumbling, and present us faultless before the presence of His glory, to the only wise God, our Saviour, be glory, and majesty, dominion and power, both now and forever. Amen."

What to do we often wonder,

As we seek some watchword true,

Lo, the answer God has given,

What would Jesus do?

When the shafts of fierce temptation,

With their fiery darts pursue,

This will be your heavenly armor,

What would Jesus do?

MARCH 30.

"I wish above all things that thou mayest prosper and be in health even as thy soul prospereth" (III. John 2).

In the way of righteousness is life and in the pathway thereof is no death. That is the secret of healing. Be right with God. Keep so. Live in the consciousness of it, and nothing can hurt you. Off from the breastplate of righteousness will glance all of the fiery darts of the devil, and faith be stronger for every fierce assault. How true it is, "Who is he that shall harm you if ye be followers of that which is good?" And how true also, "Holding faith and a good conscience, which some having put away, concerning faith, have made shipwreck."

And yet again, "If thou wilt diligently hearken to the voice of the Lord thy God, and wilt keep all His statutes and commandments, I will put none of these diseases upon thee that I have brought upon the Egyptians; for I am the Lord that healeth thee."

There's a question God is asking

Every conscience in His sight,

Let it search thine inmost being,

Is it right with God, all right?

MARCH 31.

"What things soever ye desire when ye pray, believe that ye receive them and ye shall have them" (Mark xi. 24).

Faith is not working up by will power a sort of certainty that something is coming to pass, but it is seeing as an actual fact that God has said that this thing shall come to pass, and that it is true, and then rejoicing to know that it is true, and just resting and entering into it because God has said it. Faith turns the promise into a prophecy. While it is merely a promise it is contingent upon our co-operation; it may or may not be. But when faith claims it, it becomes a prophecy and we go forth feeling that it is something that must be done because God cannot lie.

Faith is the answer from the throne saying, "It is done." Faith is the echo of God's voice. Let us catch it from on high. Let us repeat it, and go out to triumph in its glorious power.

Hear the answer from the throne,

Claim the promise, doubting one,

God hath spoken, "It is done."

Faith hath answered, "It is done";

Prayer is over, praise begun,

Hallelujah! It is done.

APRIL 1.

"Vessels of mercy which he had afore prepared unto glory" (Rom. ix. 23).

Our Father is fitting us for eternity. A vessel fitted for the kitchen will find itself in the kitchen. A vessel for the art gallery or the reception room will generally find itself there at last.

What are you getting fitted for? To be a slop-pail to hold all the stuff that people pour into your ears, or a vase to hold sweet fragrance and flowers for the King's palace and a harp of many strings that sounds the melodies and harmonies of His love and praise? Each one of us is going to his own place. Let us get fitted now.

The days of heaven are Christly days,

The Light of Heaven is He;

So walking at His side, our days

As the days of heaven would be.

The days of heaven are endless days--

Days of eternity;

55

So may our lives and works endure

While the days of heaven shall be.

Walk with us, Lord, through all the days,

And let us walk with Thee;

'Til as Thy will is done in heaven,

On earth so shall it be.

APRIL 2.

"He shall dwell on high" (Isa. xxxiii. 16).

It is easier for a consecrated Christian to live an out and out life for God than to live a mixed life. A soul redeemed and sanctified by Christ is too large for the shoals and sands of a selfish, worldly, sinful life. The great steamship, St. Paul, could sail in deep water without an effort, but she could make no progress in the shallow pool, or on the Long Branch sands; the smallest tugboat is worth a dozen of her there; but out in mid-ocean she could distance them in an hour.

Beloved, your life is too large, too glorious, too divine for the small place that you are trying to live in. Your purpose is too petty; arise and dwell on high in the resurrection life of Jesus, and the inspiring hope of His blessed coming.

Rise with thy risen Lord,

Ascend with Christ above,

And in the heavenlies walk with Him,

Whom seeing not, you love.

Walk as a heavenly race,

Princes of royal blood;

Walk as the children of the light,

The sons and heirs of God.

APRIL 3.

"My expectation is from Him" (Ps. lxii. 5).

When we believe for a blessing, we must take the attitude of faith, and begin to act and pray as if we had our blessing. We must treat God as if He had given us our request. We must lean our weight over upon Him for the thing that we have claimed, and just take it for granted that He gives it, and is going to continue to give it. This is the attitude of trust. When the wife is married, she at once falls into a new attitude, and acts in accordance with the fact, and so when

56

we take Christ as a Saviour, as a Sanctifier, as a Healer, or as a Deliverer, He expects us to fall into the attitude of recognizing Him in the capacity that we have claimed, and expect Him to be to us all that we have trusted Him for.

You may bring Him ev'ry care and burden,
You may tell Him ev'ry need in pray'r,
You may trust Him for the darkest moment,
He is caring, wherefore need you care?

Faith can never reach its consummation,
'Til the victor's thankful song we raise:
In the glorious city of salvation,
God has told us all the gates are praise.

APRIL 4.

"Resist the devil and he will flee" (James iv. 7).

Resist the devil, and he will flee from you. This is a promise, and God will keep it to us. If we resist the adversary, He will compel him to flee, and will give us the victory. We can, at all times, fearlessly stand up in defiance, in resistance to the enemy, and claim the protection of our heavenly King just as a citizen would claim the protection of the government against an outrage or injustice on the part of violent men. At the same time we are not to stand on the adversary's ground anywhere by any attitude or disobedience, or we give him a terrible power over us, which, while God will restrain in great mercy and kindness, He will not fully remove until we get fully on holy ground. Therefore, we must be armed with the breastplate of righteousness, as well as the shield of faith, if we would successfully resist the prince of darkness and the principalities in heavenly places.

Your full redemption rights
With holy boldness claim,
And to the utmost fulness prove
The power of Jesus' name.

APRIL 5.

"Many shall be purified and made white and tried" (Dan. xii. 10).

This is the promise for the Lord's coming. It is more than purity. It is to be made white, lustrous, or bright. To be purified is to have the sin burned out; to be made white is to have the glory of the Lord burned in. The one is cleansing, the other is illumination and glorification. The Lord has both for us, but in order for us to have both, we must be put into the fire to be tried, and to be led into difficult and peculiar places where Christ shall be more to us because of the very extremity of the situation. We are approaching these days. Indeed, they are already around us, and they are the precursors of the Lord's coming.

Blessed is he that keepeth his garments lest he walk naked.

There are voices in the air, filling men with hope and fear; There are signals everywhere that the end is drawing near,

There are warnings to prepare, for the King will soon be here; O it must be the coming of the Lord!

APRIL 6.

"As we have many members in one body, so we being many are one body in Christ" (Rom. xii. 4, 5).

Sometimes our communion with God is cut off, or interrupted because of something wrong with a brother, or some lack of unity in the body of Christ. We try to get at the Lord, but we cannot, because we are separated from some member of the Lord's body, or because there is not the freedom of His love flowing through every organic part. It does not need a blow upon the head to paralyze the brain; a blow upon some nerve may do it; or a wound in some artery at the extremities may be fatal to the heart. Therefore we must stand right with all His children, and meet in the body of Christ in the sweetest, fullest fellowship, if we would keep our perfect communion with Christ Himself. Sometimes we will find that an altered attitude to one Christian will bring us into the flood-tides of the Holy Ghost. It seems impossible to have faith without love, or to have Christ alone without the fulness of fellowship with all His dear saints; and if one member suffer, all suffer together, and if one rejoice, all are blessed in common.

APRIL 7.

"In Him we live and move" (Acts xvii. 28).

The hand of Gehazi, and even the staff of Elisha could not heal the lifeless boy. It needed the living touch of the prophet's own divinely quickened flesh to infuse vitality into the cold clay. Lip to lip, hand to hand, heart to heart, he must touch the child ere life could thrill his pulseless veins.

58

We must come into personal contact with the risen Saviour, and have His very life quicken our mortal flesh before we can know the fulness and reality of His healing. This is the most frequent cause of failure. People are often trusting to something that has been done to them, to something that they have done, or something that they have believed intellectually; but their spirit has not felt its way to the heart of Christ, and they have not drawn His love into their being by the hunger and thirst of love and faith, and so they are not quickened. The greatest need of our souls and bodies is to know Jesus personally, to touch Him constantly, to abide in Him continually.

May we this day lay aside all things that could hinder our near approach to Him, and walk hand in hand, heart to heart, with Jesus.

APRIL 8.

"A merry heart doeth good like a medicine" (Prov. xvii. 22).

King Solomon left among his wise sayings a prescription for sick and sad hearts, and it is one that we can safely take. "A merry heart doeth good like a medicine." Joy is the great restorer and healer. Gladness of spirit will bring health to the bones and vitality to the nerves when all other tonics fail, and all other sedatives cease to quiet. Sick one, begin to rejoice in the Lord, and your bones will flourish like an herb, and your cheeks will glow with the bloom of health and freshness. Worry, fear, distrust, care, are all poison drops; joy is balm and healing; and if you will but rejoice, God will give power. He has commanded you to be glad and rejoice; and He never fails to sustain His children in keeping His commandments. Rejoice in the Lord always, He says; which means no matter how sad, how tempted, how sick, how suffering you are, rejoice in the Lord just where you are, and begin this moment.

The joy of the Lord is the strength of our body,

The gladness of Jesus, the balm for our pain,

His life and His fulness, our fountain of healing,

His joy, our elixir for body and brain.

APRIL 9.

"I do always those things that please Him" (John viii. 29).

It is a good thing to keep short accounts with God. We were very much struck some years ago with an interpretation of this verse: "So every one of us shall give an account of himself to God." The thought conveyed to our mind was, that of accounting to God every day of our lives, so that our accounts were settled daily, and for us judgment was passed, as we lay down on our pillows every night.

This is surely the true way to live. It is the secret of great peace, and it will be a delightful comfort when life is closing, or the Master coming, to know that our account is settled, and our judgment over, and for us there is only waiting the glad "Well done, good and faithful servant, enter thou into the joy of thy Lord."

Step by step I'll walk with Jesus,

Just a moment at a time,

Heights I have not wings to soar to,

Step by step my feet can climb.

Jesus, keep me closer--closer,

Step by step and day by day

Stepping in Thy very foot-prints,

Walking with Thee all the way.

APRIL 10.

"Hold fast the confidence" (Heb. iii. 6).

Seldom have we seen a sadder wreck of even the highest, noblest Christian character than when the enemy has succeeded in undermining the simple trust of a child of God, and got him into self-accusing and condemnation. It is a fearful place when the soul allows Satan to take the throne and act as God, sitting in judgment on its every thought and act; and keeping it in the darkness of ceaseless condemnation. Well indeed has the apostle told us to hold firmly the shield of faith!

This is Satan's objective point in all his attacks upon you, to destroy your trust. If he can get you to lose your simple confidence in God, he knows that he will soon have you at his feet.

It is enough to wreck both the reason and the life for the soul that has known the sweetness of His love to lose its perfect trust in God. "Beloved, hold fast your confidence and the rejoicing of your hope firm unto the end."

Fear not to take your place

With Jesus on the throne,

And bid the powers of earth and hell,

His sovereign sceptre own.

APRIL 11.

"Commit thy way unto the Lord" (Ps. xxxvii. 5).

Seldom have we heard a better definition of faith than was given once in one of our meetings by a dear old colored woman, as she answered the question of a young man how to take the Lord for needed help.

In her characteristic way, pointing her finger toward him, she said with great emphasis: "You've just got to believe that He's done it, and it's done." The great danger with most of us is, that after we ask Him to do it, we do not believe that it's done, but we keep on helping Him, and getting others to help Him; superintending God and waiting to see how He is going to do it.

Faith adds its amen to God's yea, and then takes its hands off, and leaves God to finish His work. Its language is, "Commit thy way unto the Lord, trust also in Him; and He worketh."

Lord, I give up the struggle,

To Thee commit my way,

I trust Thy word forever,

And settle it all to-day.

APRIL 12.

"They were as it were, complainers" (Num. xi. 1).

There is a very remarkable phrase in the book of Numbers, in the account of the murmuring of the children of Israel in the wilderness. It reads like this: "When the people, as it were, murmured." Like most marginal readings it is better than the text, and a great world of suggestive truth lies back of that little sentence.

In the distance we may see many a vivid picture rise before our imagination of people who do not dare to sin openly and unequivocally, but manage to do it "as it were" only. They do not lie straight, but they evade or equivocate, or imply enough falsehood to escape a real conviction of conscience. They do not openly accuse God of unkindness or unfaithfulness, but they strike at Him through somebody else. They find fault with circumstances and people and things that God has permitted to come into their lives, and, "As it were," murmur. They do not perhaps go any farther. They feel like doing it if they dared to "charge God foolishly."

These things were written for our warning.

APRIL 13.

"Rejoice evermore" (I. Thess. v. 16).

Do not lose your joy whatever else you lose. Keep the spirit of spring. "Rejoice evermore," and "Again I say, rejoice."

The loss of Canaan began in the spirit of murmurings, "When the people, as it were, murmured, it displeased the Lord." The first break in their fellowship, the first falter in their advance, came when they began to doubt, and grieve, and fret.

Oh, keep the heart from the perforations of depression, discouragement, distrust and gloom, for Satan cannot crush a rejoicing and praiseful soul.

Look out for the beginning of sin. Don't let the first touch of evil be harbored. It is the first step that loses all. Oh, to keep so encased in the Holy Ghost and in the very life of Jesus that the evil cannot reach us!

The little fly on the inside of the window-pane may be attacked by the little bird on the outside, and it may seem to him that he is lost, but the crystal pane between keeps him safely from all danger as certainly as if it were a mighty wall of iron.

APRIL 14.

"I if I be lifted up from the earth will draw all men unto Me" (John xii. 32).

A true and pure Christian life attracts the world. There are hundreds of men and women who find no inducements whatever in the lives of ordinary Christians to interest them in practical religion, but who are won at once by a true and victorious example. We believe that more men of the world step at a bound right into a life of entire consecration than into the intermediate state which is usually presented to them at the first stage.

In an audience once there was a man who for half a century or more had lived without Christ, and who was a very prominent citizen, a man in public life, of irreproachable character, lofty intellect, and a most winning spirit and manners, but utterly out of sympathy with the Christian life.

At the close of a service for the promotion of deeper spiritual life he rose to ask the prayers of the congregation, and before the end of the week he was

himself a true and acknowledged follower of the Lord Jesus Christ. He said, as he
went home that night, "If that is the religion of Jesus Christ, I want it."

APRIL 15.

"Rooted and grounded in love" (Eph. iii. 17).

There is a very singular shrub, which grows abundantly in the west, and is to
be found in all parts of Texas. It is no less than the "mosquito tree." It is a very
slim, and willowy looking shrub, and would seem to be of little use for any
industrial purposes; but is has extraordinary roots growing like great timbers
underground, and possessing such qualities of endurance in all situations that it is
used and very highly valued for good pavements. The city of San Antonio is said
to be paved with these roots. It reminds one of those Christians who make little
show externally, but their growth is chiefly underground--out of sight, in the
depth of God. These are the men and women that God uses for the foundation of
things, and for the pavements of that city of God which will stand when all
earthly things have crumbled into ruin and dissolved into oblivion.

Deeper, deeper let the living waters flow;
Blessed Holy Spirit! River of Salvation!

All Thy fulness let me know.

APRIL 16.

"Quit you like men" (I. Cor. xvi. 13).

Be brave. Cowards always get hurt. Brave men generally come out unharmed.
Jeremiah was a hero. He shrank from nothing. He faced his king and countrymen
with dauntless bravery, and the result was he suffered no harm, but came through
the siege of Jerusalem without a hair being injured. Zedekiah, the cowardly king,
was always afraid to obey God and be true, and the result was that he at last met
the most cruel punishment that was ever inflicted on human heart.

The men and women that stand from the beginning true to their convictions
have the fewest tests. When God gives to you a good trial, if you can stand the
strain, He is not always repeating it. When Abraham offered up his son Isaac at
Mount Moriah, it was a final testing for the rest of his life. Do not let Satan see
that you are afraid of him, for he will pursue to the death if he thinks that he has a
chance of getting you.

Be true, be true,

Whether friends be false or few,

Whatsoe'er betide, ever at His side,

Let Him always find you true.

APRIL 17.

"He that ruleth his spirit is better than he that taketh a city" (Prov. xvi. 32).

Temperance is true self-government. It involves the grace of self-denial and the spirit of a sound mind. It is that poise of spirit that holds us quiet, self-possessed, recollected, deliberate, and subject ever to the voice of God and the conviction of duty in every step we take. Many persons have not that poise and recollected spirit. They are drifting at the impulse of their own impressions, moods, the influence of others, or the circumstances around them. No desire should ever control us. No purpose, however right, should have such mastery over us that we are not perfectly free. The pure affection may be an inordinate affection. Our work itself may be a selfish passion. That thing that we began to do because it was God's will, we may cling to and persist in ultimately, because it is our own will. Lord, give us the spirit ever controlled by Thy Spirit and will, and the eye that looks to Thee every moment as the eyes of a servant to the hands of her mistress. So shall Thy service be our perfect freedom, and our subjection divinest liberty.

APRIL 18.

"They shall mount up with wings" (Isa. xl. 31).

"They shall mount up with wings as eagles," is God's preliminary; for the next promise is, "They shall run and not be weary, and they shall walk and not faint." Hours of holy exultation are necessary for hours of patient plodding, waiting and working. Nature has its springs, and so has grace.

Let us rejoice in the Lord evermore, and again we say, rejoice. And let us take Him to be our continual joy, whose heart is a fountain of blessedness, and who is anointed with the oil of gladness above His fellows. We must not be disappointed if the tides are not always equally high. Even at low tide the ocean is just as full. Human nature could not stand perpetual excitement, even of a happy kind, and God often rests in His love. Let us live as self-unconsciously as possible, filling up each moment with faithful service, and trusting Him to stir the springs at His will, and as we go on in faithful service we shall hear, again and again, His glad whisper: "Well done, good and faithful servant, enter thou into the joy of thy Lord."

APRIL 19.

"Rest in the Lord and wait patiently for Him" (Ps. xxxvii. 7).

It is a very suggestive thought that it is in the Gospel of Mark, which is the Gospel of service, we hear the Master saying to His disciples, "Come ye apart into a desert place, and rest awhile." God wants rested workers. There is an energy that may be tireless and ceaseless, and yet still as the ocean's depth, with the peace of God, which passes all understanding. The two deepest secrets of rest are, first, to be in harmony with the will of God, and, secondly, to trust. "Great peace have they that love Thy law," expresses the first. "Thou will keep him in perfect peace whose mind is stayed on Thee, because he trusteth in Thee," describes the second. There is a good deal in learning to "stay." Sometimes we forget that it literally means to stop. It is a great blessing even to stop all thought, and this is frequently the only way to answer the devil's whirlwind of irritating questions and thoughts, to be absolutely still and refuse to even think, and meet his evil voice with a simple and everlasting "No!" If we will be still God will give us peace.

APRIL 20.

"There they dwelt with the King for His work" (I. Chron. iv. 23).

It is easy for water to run down from the upper springs, but it requires a divine impulse to flow up from the valley in the nether springs. There is nothing that tells more of Christ than to see a Christian rejoicing and cheerful in the humdrum and routine of commonplace work, like the sailors that stand on the dock loading the vessel and singing as they swing their loads, keeping time with the spirit of praise to the footsteps and movements of labor and duty. No one has a sweeter or higher ministry for Christ than a business man or a serving woman who can carry the light of heaven in their faces all day long. Like the sea fowl that can plunge beneath the briny tide with its beautiful and spotless plumage, and come forth without one drop adhering to its burnished breast and glowing wings because of the subtle oil upon the plumage that keeps the water from sticking, so, thank God, we too may be so anointed with the Holy Ghost that sin, sorrow and defilement will not adhere to us, but we shall pass through every sea as the ship passes through the waves, in, but above the floods around us.

APRIL 21.

"The anointing which ye have received" (I. John ii. 27).

This is the secret of the deeper life, but "That ye may be rooted and grounded in love," is the substance of it, and the sweetness of it. The fulness of the divine love in the heart will make everything easy. It is very easy to do things that we love to do, and it is very easy to trust one whom we love, and the more we realize their love the more we will trust them for it. It is the source of healing. The tide of love flowing through our bodies will strangely strengthen our very frame, and the love of our Lord will become a continual spring of youth and freshness in our physical being. The secret of love is very simple. It is to take the heart of Jesus for our love and claim its love for every need of life, whether it be toward God or toward others. It is very sweet to think of persons in this way, "I will take the heart of Jesus toward them, to let me love them as He loves them." Then we can love even the unworthy in some measure, if we shall see them in the light of His love and hope, as they shall be, and not as they now are, unworthy of our love.

APRIL 22.

"Christ is the head" (Eph. v. 23).

Often we want people to pray for us and help us, but always defeat our object when we look too much to them and lean upon them. The true secret of union is for both to look upon God, and in the act of looking past themselves to Him they are unconsciously united. The sailor was right when he saw the little boy fall overboard and waited a minute before he plunged to his rescue. When the distracted mother asked him in agony why he had waited so long, he sensibly replied: "I knew that if I went in before he would clutch and drag me down. I waited until his struggles were over, and then I was able to help him when he did not grasp me too strongly."

When people grasp us too strongly, either with their love or with their dependence, we are intuitively conscious that they are not looking to God, and we become paralyzed in our efforts to help them. United prayer, therefore, requires that the one for whom we pray be looking away from us to the Lord Jesus Christ, and we together look to Him alone.

66

APRIL 23.

"An high priest touched with the feeling of our infirmities" (Heb. iv. 15).

Some time ago we were talking with a greatly suffering sister about healing, who was much burdened physically and desirous of being able to trust the Lord for deliverance. After a little conversation we prayed with her, committing her case to the Lord for absolute trust and deliverance as she was prepared to claim. As soon as we closed our prayer she grasped our hand, and asked us to unite with her in the burden that was most upon her heart, and then, without a word of reference to her own healing, or the burden under which she was being crushed to death, she burst into such a prayer for a poor orphan boy, of whom she had just heard that day, as we have never heard surpassed for sympathy and love, imploring God to help him and save him, and sobbing in spasmodic agony of love many times during her prayer, and then she ceased without even referring to her own need. We were deeply touched by the spectacle of love, and we thought how the Father's heart must be touched for her own need.

APRIL 24.

"Fret not thyself in any wise" (Ps. xxxvii. 8).

A life was lost in Israel because a pair of human hands were laid unbidden upon the ark of God. They were placed upon it with the best intent to steady it when trembling and shaking as the oxen drew it along the rough way, but they touched God's work presumptuously, and they fell paralyzed and lifeless. Much of the life of faith consists in letting things alone. If we wholly trust an interest to God we can keep our hands off it, and He will guard it for us better than we can help Him. "Rest in the Lord and wait patiently for Him. Fret not thyself in any wise because of him that prospereth in the way, because of the man that bringeth wicked devices to pass." Things may seem to be going all wrong, but He knows as well as we; and He will arise in the right moment if we are really trusting Him so fully as to let Him work in His own way and time. There is nothing so masterly as inactivity in some things, and there is nothing so hurtful as restless working, for God has undertaken to work His sovereign will.

APRIL 25.

"The very God of Peace sanctify you wholly" (I. Thess. v. 23).

A great tidal wave is bearing up the stranded ship, until she floats above the bar without a straining timber or struggling seaman, instead of the ineffectual and toilsome efforts of the struggling crew and the strain of the engines, which had tried in vain to move her an inch until that heavenly impulse lifted her by its own attraction.

It is God's great law of gravitation lifting up, by the warm sunbeams, the mighty iceberg which a million men could not raise a single inch, but melts away before the rays and the warmth of the sunshine, and rises in clouds of evaporation to meet its embrace until that cold and heavy mass is floating in fleecy clouds of glory in the blue ocean of the sky.

How easy all this! How mighty! How simple! How divine! Beloved, have you come into the divine way of holiness! If you have, how your heart must swell with gratitude! If you have not, do you not long for it, and will you not unite in the prayer of the text that the very God of peace will sanctify you wholly?

APRIL 26.

"Strangers and pilgrims" (Heb. xi. 13).

If you have ever tried to plough a straight furrow in the country--we are sorry for the man that does not know how to plough and more sorry for the man that is too proud to want to know--you have found it necessary to have two stakes in a line and to drive your horses by these stakes. If you have only one stake before you, you will have no steadying point for your vision, but you can wiggle about without knowing it and make your furrows as crooked as a serpent's coil; but if you have two stakes and ever keep them in line, you cannot deviate an inch from a straight line, and your furrow will be an arrow speeding to its course.

This has been a great lesson to us in our Christian life. If we would run a straight course, we find that we must have two stakes, the near and the distant. It is not enough to be living in the present, but it is a great and glorious thing to have a distant goal, a definite object, a clear purpose before us for which we are living, and unto which we are shaping our present.

APRIL 27.

"The sweetness of the lips" (Prov. xvi. 21).

Spiritual conditions are inseparably connected with our physical life. The flow of the divine life-currents may be interrupted by a little clot of blood; the vital current may leak out through a very trifling wound.

If you want to keep the health of Christ, keep from all spiritual sores, from all heart wounds and irritations. One hour of fretting will wear out more vitality than a week of work; and one minute of malignity, or rankling jealousy or envy will hurt more than a drink of poison. Sweetness of spirit and joyousness of heart are essential to full health. Quietness of spirit, gentleness, tranquility, and the peace of God that passes all understanding, are worth all the sleeping draughts in the country.

We do not wonder that some people have poor health when we hear them talk for half an hour. They have enough dislikes, prejudices, doubts, and fears to exhaust the strongest constitution.

Beloved, if you would keep God's life and strength, keep out the things that kill it; keep it for Him, and for His work, and you will find enough and to spare.

APRIL 28.

"For it is God which worketh in you" (Phil. ii. 13).

Sanctification is the gift of the Holy Ghost, the fruit of the Spirit, the grace of the Lord Jesus Christ, the prepared inheritance of all who enter in, the greatest obtainment of faith, not the attainment of works. It is divine holiness, not human self-improvement, nor perfection. It is the inflow into man's being of the life and purity of the infinite, eternal and Holy One, bringing His own perfection and working out His own will. How easy, how spontaneous, how delightful this heavenly way of holiness! Surely it is a "highway" and not the low way of man's vain and fruitless mortification.

It is God's great elevated railway, sweeping over the heads of the struggling throngs who toil along the lower pavement when they might be borne along on His ascension pathway, by His own almighty impulse. It is God's great elevator carrying us up to the higher chambers of His palace, without over-laborious efforts, while others struggle up the winding stairs and faint by the way.

Let us to-day so fully take Him that He can "cause us to walk in His statutes."

APRIL 29.

"Love never faileth" (I. Cor. xiii. 8).

In our work for God it is a great thing to find the key to men's hearts, and recognize something good as a point of contact for our spiritual influence. When Jesus met the woman at Samaria He immediately seized hold of the best things in her, and by this He reached her heart, and drew from her a willing confession of her salvation. A Scotchman once said that his salvation was all due to the fact that a good man (Lord Shaftsbury, we believe) once put his arms around him and said, "John, by the grace of God we will make a man of you yet."

The old legend tells the story of a poor, dead dog lying on the street in the midst of the crowd, every one of whom was having something to say, until Jesus came along, and immediately began to admire its beautiful teeth. He had something kind to say even of him.

There is but One can live and love like this;

The Christ-love from the living Christ must spring.

O! Jesus! come and live Thy life in me,

And all Thy heaven of love and blessing bring.

APRIL 30.

"Love believeth all things" (I. Cor. xiii. 7).

Beautiful is the expression in the Book of Isaiah which reflects with exceeding sweetness the love of our dear Lord. He said, "They are My people, children that will not lie; so He was their Saviour." They did lie, but He would not believe it. At least He speaks as if He would not believe it in the greatness of His love, because they were His people. He has not seen iniquity in Jacob nor perversity in Israel. There is plenty of it to see, and the devil sees it all, and a good many people are only too glad to see it; but the dear Father will not see it. He covers it with His love and the precious blood of His dear atoning Son. Such a wonderful love ought surely to make us gentler to others, and more anxious to cause our Father less need to hide His loving eyes from our imperfections and faults.

If we have the mind and heart of Christ, we shall clothe even the world with those graces which faith can claim for them, and try our best to count them as if they were real, and by love and prayer we shall at length make them real. "Love believeth all things."

MAY 1.

"The fruit of the Spirit is gentleness" (Gal. v. 22).

Nature's harshness has melted away and she is now beaming with the smile of spring, and everything around us whispers of the gentleness of God. This beautiful fruit is in lovely harmony with the gentle month of which it is the keynote. May the Holy Spirit lead us, beloved, these days, into His sweetness, quietness, and gentleness, subduing every coarse, rude, harsh, and unholy habit, and making us like Him, of whom it is said, "He shall not strive, nor cry, nor cause His voice to be heard in the streets."

The man who is truly filled with Jesus will always be a gentleman. The woman who is baptized of the Holy Ghost, will have the instincts of a perfect lady, although low born and little bred in the schools of earthly refinement. Beloved, let us receive and reflect the gentleness of Christ, the spirit of the holy babe, until the world will say of us, as the polished and infidel Chesterfield once said of the saintly Fenelon, "If I had remained in his house another day, I should have had to become a Christian."

Lord, help us to-day, to so yield to the gentle Dove-Spirit, that our lives shall be as His life.

MAY 2.

"Always causeth us to triumph" (II. Cor. ii. 14).

How these words help us. Think of them when the people rasp you, when the devil pricks you with his fiery darts, when your sensitive, self-willed spirit chafes or frets; let a gentle voice be heard above the strife, whispering, "Keep sweet, keep sweet!" And, if you will but heed it quickly, you will be saved from a thousand falls and kept in perfect peace.

True, you cannot keep yourself sweet, but God will keep you if He sees that it is your fixed, determined purpose to be kept sweet, and to refuse to fret or grudge or retaliate. The trouble is, you rather enjoy a little irritation and morbidness. You want to cherish the little grudge, and sympathize with your hurt feelings, and nurse your little grievance.

Dear friends, God will give you all the love you really want and honestly choose. You can have your grievance or you can have the peace that passeth all understanding; but you cannot have both.

There is a balm for a thousand heartaches, and a heaven of peace and power in these two little words--KEEP SWEET.

MAY 3.

"My peace I give unto you" (John xiv. 27).

Here lies the secret of abiding peace--God's peace. We give ourselves to God and the Holy Spirit takes possession of our breast. It is indeed "Peace, Peace." But it is just then that the devil begins to turn us away, and he does it through our thoughts, diverting or distracting them as occasion requires. This is the time to prove the sincerity of our consecration and the singleness of our heart. If we truly desire His Presence more than all else, we will turn away from every conflicting thought and look steadily up to Jesus. But if we desire the gratification of our impulse more than His Presence, we will yield to the passionate word or the frivolous thought or the sinful diversion, and when we come back our Shepherd has gone, and we wonder why our peace has departed. Failure occurs often in some trifling thing, and the soul failure has occurred in some trifling thing, usually a thought or word, and the soul which would not have feared to climb a mountain has really stumbled over a straw.

The real secret of perfect rest is to be jealously, habitually occupied with Jesus.

MAY 4.

"Greater is He that is in you than he that is in the world" (I. John iv. 4).

Satan loves to trip us over little things. The reason of this is because it is generally a greater victory for him, and shows that he can upset us by a shaving and knock us down with a straw. It is the old boast of the Jebusite, when they told David they could defend Jerusalem by a garrison of the blind and lame. Most of us get on better in our great struggles than we do in our little ones. It was over a little apple that Adam fell, but all the world was wrecked. Look out, beloved, for the little stumbling blocks, and do not let Satan laugh at you, and tell his myrmidons how he tripped you over an orange peel. And, too, when the devil wants to stop some great blessing in our lives, he generally throws some ugly shadow over it and makes it look distasteful to us. How many of us have been keeping back from truths, places and persons in which God has reappeared, the greatest blessing of our lives, and the devil has succeeded in keeping us away from them by some false or foolish prejudice!

MAY 5.

"If ye then be risen" (Col. iii. 1).

God is waiting this morning to mark the opening hours for every ready and willing heart with a touch of life and power that will lift our lives to higher pleasures and offer to our vision grander horizons of hope and holy service.

We shall not need to seek far to discover our risen Lord. He was in advance even of the earliest seeker that Easter morning, and He will be waiting for us before the break of day with His glad "All Hail," if we have only eyes to see and hearts to welcome and obey Him.

What is His message to us this spring time? "If ye then be risen with Christ, seek those things which are above, where Christ sitteth on the right hand of God. For ye are dead, and your life is hid with Christ in God."

It is not risen with Christ, but _resurrected_. It is not rising a little higher in the old life, but it is rising from the dead. The resurrection will mean no more than the death has meant. Only so far as we are really dead shall we live with Him.

MAY 6.

"Reckon ye also yourselves to be alive unto God" (Rom. vi. 11).

Death is but for a moment. Life is forevermore. Live, then, ye children of the resurrection, on His glorious life, more and more abundantly, and the fulness of your life will repel the intrusion of self and sin, and overcome evil with good, and your existence will be, not the dreary repression of your own struggling, but the springing tide of Christ's spontaneous overcoming life.

Once in a religious meeting a dear brother gave us a most exhilarating talk on the risen life. Then another brother got up and talked for a long time on the necessity of self-crucifixion. A cold sweat fell over us all, and we could scarcely understand why. But after he had got through, a good sister clarified the whole situation by saying, that "Pastor S. had taken us all out of the grave by his address, and then Pastor P. has put us back again."

Don't go back into the grave again after you have got out, but live like Him, who "liveth and was dead, and lo! He is alive forevermore, and has the keys of hell and of death." Keep out of the tomb, and keep the door locked, and the keys in His risen hands.

MAY 7.

"I travail in birth again until Christ be formed in you" (Gal. iv. 19).

It is a blessed moment when we are born again and a new heart is created in us after the image of God. It is a more blessed moment when in this new heart Christ Himself is born and the Christmas time is reproduced in us as we, in some real sense, become incarnations of the living Christ. This is the deepest and holiest meaning of Christianity. It is expressed in Paul's prayer for the Galatians. "My little children, for whom I travail in birth again till Christ be formed in you."

There will yet be a more glorious era when we, like Him, shall be transformed and transfigured into His glory, and in the resurrection shall be, in spirit, soul and body, even as He.

Let us live, under the power of the inspiring thought, incarnations of Christ; not living our life, but the Christ-life, and showing forth the excellencies, not of ourselves, but of Him who hath called us "out of darkness into His marvelous light"; so our life shall be to all the re-living in our position of the Christ life, as He would have lived it, had He been here.

MAY 8.

"Except a corn of wheat fall into the ground and die" (John xii. 24).

Death and resurrection are the central ideas of nature and Christianity. We see them in the transformation of the chrysalis, in the buried seed bursting into the bud and blossom of the spring, in the transformation of the winding sheet of winter to the many tinted robes of spring. We see it all through the Bible in the symbol of circumcision, with its significance of death and life, in the passage of the Red Sea and the Jordan leading out and leading in, and in the Cross of Calvary and the open grave of the Easter morning. We see it in every deep spiritual life. Every true life is death-born, and the deeper the dying the truer the living. We doubt not the months that have been passing have shown us all many a place where there ought to be a grave, and many a lingering shred of the natural and sinful which we would gladly lay down in a bottomless grave. God help us to pass the irrevocable sentence of death and to let the Holy Ghost, the great undertaker, make the interment eternal. Then our life shall be ever budding and blossoming and shedding fragrance over all.

MAY 9.

"All hail" (Matt. xxviii. 9).

It was a stirring greeting which the Lord of Life spake to His first disciples on the morning of the resurrection. It is a bright and radiant word which in His name we would speak to His beloved children at the commencement of another day. It means a good deal more than appears on the surface. It is really a prayer for our health, but which none but those who believe in the healing of the body can fully understand. A thoughtful friend suggested once that the word "hail" really means health, and it is just the old Saxon form of the word. We all know that a hale person is a healthy person. Our Lord's message, therefore, was substantially that greeting which from time immemorial we give to one another when we meet. "How is your health?" "How are you?" or, better still, "I wish you health." Christ's wish is tantamount to a promise and command. It is very similar to the Apostle John's benediction to his dear friend Gaius, and we would re-echo it to our beloved friends according to the fulness of the Master's will.

MAY 10.

"I am alive forevermore" (Rev. i. 18).

Here is the message of the Christ of the cross and the still more glorious and precious Christ of the resurrection. It is beautiful and inspiring to note the touch of light and glory with which these simple words invest the cross. It is not said I am He that was dead and liveth, but "I am He that liveth and was dead, but am alive forevermore." Life is mentioned before the death. There are two ways of looking at the cross. One is from the death side and the other from the life side. One is the Ecce Homo and the other is the glorified Jesus with only the marks of the nails and the spear. It is thus we are to look at the cross. We are not to carry about with us the mould of the sepulchre, but the glory of the resurrection. It is not the Ecce Homo, but the Living Christ. And so our crucifixion is to be so complete that it shall be lost in our resurrection and we shall even forget our sorrow and carry with us the light and glory of the eternal morning. So let us live the death-born life, ever new and full of a life that can never die, because it is "dead and alive forevermore."

MAY 11.

"Whosoever will save his life shall lose it" (Luke ix. 24).

First and foremost Christ teaches resurrection and life. The power of Christianity is life. It brings us not merely law, duty, example, with high and holy teaching and admonition. It brings us the power to follow the higher ideal and the life that spontaneously does the things commanded. But it is not only life, but resurrection life.

And it begins with a real crisis, a definite transaction, a point of time as clear as the morning dawn. It is not an everlasting dying and an eternal struggle to live. But it is all expressed in a tense that denotes definiteness, fixedness and finished action. We actually died at a certain point and as actually began to live the resurrection life.

Let us reckon ourselves to be dead indeed unto sin, but alive unto God through Jesus Christ.

And death is only the pathway and portal,
To the life that shall die nevermore;
And the cross leadeth up to the crown everlasting,
The Jordan to Canaan's bright shore.

MAY 12.

"Tell me where Thou makest Thy flock to rest at noon" (Song of Solomon i. 7).

Beloved, do you not long for God's quiet, the inner chambers, the shadow of the Almighty, the secret of His presence? Your life has been, perhaps, all driving and doing, or perhaps straining, struggling, longing and not obtaining. Oh, for rest! to lie down upon His bosom and know that you have all in Him, that every question is answered, every doubt settled, every interest safe, every prayer answered, every desire satisfied. Lift up the cry, "Tell me, O Thou whom my soul loveth, where Thou feedest, where Thou makest Thy flock to rest at noon"!

Blessed be His name! He has this for us, His exclusive love--a love which each individual somehow feels is all for himself, in which he can lie alone upon His breast and have a place which none other can dispute; and yet His heart is so great that He can hold a thousand millions just as near, and each heart seem to possess Him just as exclusively for his own, even as the thousand little pools of water upon the beach can reflect the sun, and each little pool seems to have the whole sun embosomed in its beautiful depths. And Christ can teach us this secret of His inmost love.

MAY 13.

"Abide in Me" (John xv. 4).

Christianity may mean nothing more than a religious system. Christian life may mean nothing more than an earnest and honest attempt to follow and imitate Christ.

Christ life is more than these, and expresses our actual union with the Lord Jesus Christ, and He is undoubtedly in us as the life and source of all our experience and work.

This conception of the highest Christian life is at once simpler and sublimer than any other. We do not teach in these pages, that the purpose of Christ's redemption is to restore us to Adamic perfection, for if we had it we should lose it to-morrow; but rather to unite us with the Second Adam, and lift us up to a higher plane than our first parents ever knew.

This is the only thing that can reconcile the warring elements of diverse schools of teaching with respect to Christian life.

The Spirit of God will lead us to have no controversy respecting mere theories, but simply hold to the person and life of Jesus Christ Himself, and the privilege of being united to Him, and living in constant dependence upon His keeping power and grace.

MAY 14.

"But God" (Luke xii. 20).

What else do we really need? What else is He trying to make us understand? The religion of the Bible is wholly supernatural. The one resource of faith has always been the living God, and Him alone. The children of Israel were utterly dependent upon Jehovah as they marched through the wilderness, and the one reason their foes feared them and hastened to submit themselves was that they recognized among them the shout of a King, and the presence of One compared with whom all their strength was vain.

"Wherein," asked Moses, "shall we be separated from all other peoples of the earth, except it be in this that Thou goest before us."

A church relying on human wisdom, wealth or resources, ceases to be the body of Christ and becomes an earthly society. When we dare to depend entirely upon God and without doubt, the humblest and feeblest agencies will become "mighty through God, to the pulling down of strongholds." May the Holy Spirit give to us at all times, His own conception of these two great words, "But God."

MAY 15.

"I press toward the mark" (Phil. iii. 14).

We have thought much about what we have received. Let us think of the things we have not received, of some of the vessels that have not yet been filled, of some of the places in our life that the Holy Ghost has not yet possessed for God, and signalized by His glory and His presence.

Shall the coming months be marked by a diligent, heart-searching application of "the rest of the oil," to the yet unoccupied possibilities of our life and service?

Have we known His fulness of grace in our spiritual life? Have we tasted a little of His glory? Have we believed His promise for the mind, the soul, the spirit? Have we known all His possibilities for the body? Have we tested Him in His power to control the events of providence, and to move the hearts of men and nations? Has He opened to us the treasure-house of God, and met our financial needs as He might? Have we even begun to understand the ministry of prayer, as God would have us exercise it? God give us "the rest of the oil"!

MAY 16.

"It is not in man that walketh to direct his steps" (Jer. x. 23).

United to Jesus Christ as your Redeemer, you are accepted in the Beloved. He does not merely take my place as a man and settle my debts. He does that and more. He comes to give a perfect ideal of what a man should be. He is the model man, not for us to copy, for that would only bring discouragement and utter failure; but He will come and copy Himself in us. If Christ lives in me, I am another Christ. I am not like Him, but I have the same mind. The very Christ is in me. This is the foundation of Christian holiness and Divine healing. Christ is developing a perfect life within us. Some say man can never be perfect. "It is not in man that walketh to direct his steps." We are all a lot of failures. This is true, but we should go further. We must take God's provision for our failure and rise above it through His grace. We must take Jesus as a substitute for our miserable self. We must give up the good as well as the bad and take Him instead. It is hard for us to learn that the very good must go, but we must have Divine impulses instead of even our best attainments.

78

MAY 17.

"To him that overcometh, will I give" (Rev. ii. 17).

A precious secret of Christian life is to have Jesus dwelling within the heart and conquering things that we never could overcome. It is the only secret of power in your life and mine, beloved. Men cannot understand it, nor will the world believe it; but it is true, that God will come to dwell within us, and be the power, and the purity, and the victory, and the joy of our life. It is no longer now, "What is the best that I can do?" but the question is, "What is the best that Christ can do?" It enables us to say, with Paul, in that beautiful passage in Philippians, "I know both how to be abased, and I know how to abound, everywhere and in all things, I am instructed both to be full and to be hungry, both to abound and to suffer need. I can do all things through Christ, which strengtheneth me."

With this knowledge I go forth to meet my testings, and the secret stands me good. It keeps me pure and sweet, as I could never keep myself. Christ has met the adversary and defeated him for me. Thanks be unto God who giveth us the victory through Jesus Christ.

MAY 18.

"For ye are dead" (Col. iii. 3).

Now, this definite, absolute and final putting off of ourselves in an act of death, is something we cannot do ourselves. It is not self-mortifying, but it is dying with Christ. There is nothing can do it but the Cross of Christ and the Spirit of God. The church is full of half dead people who have been trying, like poor Nero, to slay themselves for years, and have not had the courage to strike the fatal blow. Oh, if they would just put themselves at Jesus' feet, and let Him do it, there would be accomplishment and rest. On that cross He has provided for our death as well as our life, and our part is just to let His death be applied to our nature just as it has been to our old sins, and then leave it with Him, think no more about it, and count it dead, not recognizing it any longer as ourselves, but another, refusing to listen or fear it, to be identified with it, or even try to cleanse it, but counting it utterly in His hands, and dead to us forever, and for all our new life depending on Him at every breath, as a babe just born depends upon its mother's life.

MAY 19.

"He purgeth it that it may bring forth more fruit" (John xv. 2).

Recently we passed a garden. The gardener had just finished his pruning, and the wounds of the knife and saw were just beginning to heal, while the warm April sun was gently nourishing the stricken plant into fresh life and energy. We thought as we looked at that plant how cruel it would be to begin next week and cut it down. Now, the gardener's business is to revive and nourish it into life. Its business is not to die, but to live. So, we thought, it is with the discipline of the soul. It, too, has its dying hour; but it must not be always dying: Rather reckon ourselves to be dead indeed unto sin, but alive unto God through Jesus Christ our Lord. Death is but a moment. Live, then, ye children of the resurrection, on His glorious life more and more abundantly, and the fulness of your life will repel the intrusion of self and sin, and overcome evil with good, and your existence will be, not the dreary repression of your own struggling, but the springing tide of Christ's spontaneous overcoming and everlasting life.

MAY 20.

"Ye are not your own" (I. Cor. vi. 19).

What a privilege that we may consecrate ourselves. What a mercy that God will take us worthless worms. What rest and comfort lie hidden in those words, "Not my own." Not responsible for my salvation, not burdened by my cares, not obliged to live for my interests, but altogether His; redeemed, owned, saved, loved, kept in the strong, unchanging arms of His everlasting love. Oh, the rest from sin and self and cankering care which true consecration brings! To be able to give Him our poor weak life, with its awful possibilities and its utter helplessness, and know that He will accept it, and take a joy and pride in making out of it the utmost possibilities of blessing, power and usefulness; to give all, and find in so doing we have gained all; to be so yielded to Him in entire self surrender, that He is bound to care for us as for Himself. We are putting ourselves in the hands of a loving Father, more solicitous for our good than we can be and only wanting us to be fully submitted to Him that He may be more free to bless us.

MAY 21.

"We will come unto Him and make our abode with Him" (John xiv. 23).

80

The Bible has always held out two great promises respecting Christ. First, I will come to you; and, second, I will come into you. For four thousand years the world looked forward to the fulfilment of the first. The other is the secret which Paul says has been hid from ages and generations, but is now made manifest to His saints, which is Christ in you, the hope of glory. This is just as great a revelation of God as the incarnation of Jesus, for it makes you like Christ, as free from sin as He is. If Christ is in you, what will be the consequences? Why, He will put you aside entirely. The I in you will go. You will say, "Not I, but Christ." Christ undertakes your battles for you. Christ becomes purity and grace and strength in you. You do not try to attain unto these things, but you know you have obtained them in Him. It is glorious rest with the Master. Jesus does not say, "Now we must bring forth fruit, we must pray much, we must do this or that." There is no constraint about it, except that we must abide in Him. That is the center of all joy and help.

MAY 22.

"Fight the good fight of faith" (I. Tim. vi. 12).

Oh, beloved, how must God feel about us after He has given us His heart's blood, put so many advantages in our way, expended upon us so much grace and care, if we should disappoint Him. It makes the spirit cry, "Who is sufficient for these things?" Evermore I can see before me the time when you and I shall stand on yonder shore and look back upon the years that have been, these few short years of time. Oh, may we cast ourselves at Jesus' feet and say: "Many a time have we faltered; many a hard fight has come, but Thou hast kept me and held me, thanks to God, who has given me the victory through the Lord Jesus Christ." From the battlefields of the Peninsula, a little band of veterans came forth, and they gave each a medal with the names of all their battles on one side, and on the other side this little sentence, "I was there." Oh, when that hour shall come, may it be a glad, glad thought to look back over the trials and sacrifices of these days and remember, "I was there, and by the help of God and the grace of Jesus, I am here."

MAY 23.

"The fulness of the blessing of the Gospel of Christ" (Rom. xv. 29).

Many Christians fail to see these blessings as they are centered in Him. They want to get the blessing of salvation, but that is not the Christ. They want to get the blessing of His grace to help, but that is not Him. They want to get answered prayer from Him to work for Him. You might have all that and not have the blessing of Christ Himself. A great many people are attached rather to the system of doctrine. They say, "Yes, I have got the truth; I am orthodox." That is not the Christ. It may be the cold statue in the fountain with the water passing from the cold hands and lips, but no life there. A great many other people want to get the blessing of joy, but it is not the blessing of Christ personally. A great many people are more attached to their church and pastor, or to dear Christians friends, but that is not the Christ. The blessing that will alone fill your heart when all else fails is the loving heart of Jesus united to you, the fountain of all your blessings and the unfailing one when they all wither and are exhausted--Jesus Christ Himself.

MAY 24.

"Where is the way where light dwelleth" (Job xxxviii. 19).

Jewels, in themselves, are valueless, unless they are brought in contact with light. If they are put in certain positions they will reflect the beauty of the sun. There is no beauty in them otherwise. The diamond that is back in its dark gallery or down in the deep mine, displays no beauty whatever. What is it but a piece of charcoal, a bit of common carbon, unless it becomes a medium for reflecting light? And so it is also with the other precious gems. Their varied tints are nothing without light. If they are many-sided, they reflect more light, and display more beauty. If you put paste beside a diamond there is no brilliancy in it. In its crude state it does not reflect light at all. So we are in a crude state and are of no use at all until God comes and shines upon us. The light that is in a diamond is not its own possession; it is the beauty of the sun. What beauty is there in the child of God? Only the beauty of Jesus. We are His peculiar people, chosen to show forth His excellencies who hath called us out of darkness into His marvelous light. Let its reflect to-day His light and love.

MAY 25.

"That I may know Him" (Phil. iii. 10).

Better to know Jesus Himself than to know the truth about Him for the deep things of God as they are revealed by the Holy Ghost. It was Paul's great desire, "That I may know Him," not about Him, not the mysteries of the wonderful world, of the deeper and higher teachings of God, but to enter into the Holy of Holies, where Christ is, where the Shekinah is shining and making the place glorious with the holiness of God, and then to enter into the secret of the Lord Himself. It was what Jacob strove for at Peniel, when he pleaded with God, "Tell me Thy name." He has told us His name, giving us "the light of the knowledge of the glory of God in the face of Jesus Christ." That is the secret. It is the Lord Himself, and nothing else; it is acquaintance with God; it is knowing Jesus Christ as we know no one else; it is being able to say, not only "I believe Him," but "I know Him"; not about Him, but I know Him. That is the secret above all others that God wants us to have; it is His provision for glory and power, and it is given freely to the single-hearted seeker.

MAY 26.

"Be careful for nothing; but in everything by prayer and supplication with thanksgiving let your requests be made known unto God" (Phil. iv. 6).

Commit means to hand over, to trust wholly to another. So, if we give our trials to Him, He will carry them. If we walk in righteousness He will carry us through. "Humble yourselves, therefore, under the mighty hand of God that He may exalt you in due time." There are two hands there--God's hand pressing us down, humbling us, and then God's hand lifting us up. Cast all your care on Him, then His hand will lift you up, exalt you in due time. There are two cares in this verse--your care and His care. They are different in the original. One means anxious care, the other means Almighty care. Cast your anxious care on Him and take His Almighty care instead. Make no account of trouble any more, but believe He is able to sustain you through it. The government is on His shoulder. Believe that, if you trust and obey Him, and meet His will, He will look after your interests. Simply exchange burdens. Take His yoke upon you, and let Him care for you.

MAY 27.

"The government shall be upon His shoulder" (Isa. ix. 6).

You cannot make the heart restful by stopping its beating. Belladonna will do that, but that is not rest. Let the breath of life come--God's life and strength--and there will be sweet rest. Home ties and family affection will not bring it. Deliverance from trouble will not bring it. Many a tried heart has said: "If this great trouble was only gone, I should have rest." But as soon as one goes another comes. The poor, wounded deer on the mountain side, thinks if he could only bathe in the old mountain stream he would have rest. But the arrow is in its flesh and there is no rest for it till the wound is healed. It is as sore in the mountain lake as on the plain. We shall never have God's rest and peace in the heart till we have given everything up to Christ--even our work--and believe He has taken it all, and we have only to keep still and trust. It is necessary to walk in holy obedience and let Him have the government on His shoulder. Paul said this: "This one thing I do." There is one narrow path for us all--Christ's will and work for us.

MAY 28.

"He humbled Himself" (Phil. ii. 8).

One of the hardest things for a lofty and superior nature is to be under authority, to renounce his own will, and to take a place of subjection. But Christ took upon Him the form of a servant, gave up His independence, His right to please Himself, His liberty of choice, and after having from eternal ages known only to command, gave Himself up only to obey. I have seen occasionally the man who was once a wealthy employer a clerk in the same store. It was not an easy or graceful position, I assure you. But Jesus was such a perfect servant that His Father said: "Behold, My Servant in whom My soul delighteth." All His life His watchword was, "The Son of Man came to minister." "I am among you as He that doth serve." "I can do nothing of Myself." "Not My will, but Thine, be done." Have you, beloved, learned the servant's place?

And once more, "He became obedient unto death, even the death of the cross." His life was all a dying, and at last He gave all up to death, and also shame, the death of crucifixion. This last was the consummation of His love.

MAY 29.

"The body is for the Lord and the Lord for the body" (I. Cor. vi. 13).

Now, just as it was Christ Himself who justified us, and Christ Himself who was made unto us sanctification, so it is only by personal union with Him that we can receive this physical life and redemption. It is, indeed, not a touch of power upon our body which restores and then leaves it to the mere resources of natural strength and life for the future; but it is the vital and actual union of our mortal body with the risen body of our Lord Jesus Christ, so that His own very life comes into our frame and He is Himself made unto us strength, health and full physical redemption.

He is alive forevermore and condescends to live in these houses of clay. They who thus receive Him may know Him as none ever can who exclude Him from the bodies which He has made for Himself. This is one of the deep and precious mysteries of the Gospel. "The body is for the Lord, and the Lord for the body." "Know ye not that your body is the temple of the Holy Ghost, which is in you, and ye are not your own, for ye are bought with a price; therefore, glorify God in your body, which is God's." (R. V.)

MAY 30.

"I will put My Spirit within you" (Ez. xxxvi. 27).

"I will put My Spirit within you, and I will cause you to walk in My statutes, and ye shall keep My judgments." "I will put My fear in your hearts, and ye shall not turn away from Me." Oh, friend, would not that be blessed, would not that be such a rest for you, all worn out with this strife in your own strength? Do you not want a strong man to conquer the strong man of self and sin? Do you not want a leader? Do you not want God Himself to be with you, to be your occupant? Do you not want rest? Are you not conscious of this need? Oh, this sense of being beaten back, longing, wanting, but not accomplishing. That is what He comes to do; "Ye shall receive power after that the Holy Ghost has come upon you." Better than that, "Ye shall receive the power of the Holy Ghost coming upon you." That is the true version, and really it is immensely different from the other. You shall not receive power yourself, so that people shall say: "How much power that man has. You shall not have any power whatever, but you shall receive the power of the Holy Ghost coming upon you, He having the power, that is all."

MAY 31.

"Whosoever therefore shall humble himself as this little child" (Matt. xviii. 4).

You will never get a humble heart until it is born from above, from the heart of Christ. For man has lost his own humanity and alas, too often has a demon heart. God wants us, as Christians, to be simple, human, approachable and childlike. The Christians that we know and love best, and that are nearest to the Lord, are the most simple. Whenever we grow stilted we are only fit for a picture gallery, and we are only good on a pedestal; but, if we are going to live among men and love and save them, we must be approachable and human. All stiffness is but another form of self-consciousness. Ask Christ for a human heart, for a smile that will be as natural as your little child's in your presence. Oh, how much Christ did by little touches! He never would have got at the woman of Samaria if He had come to her as the prophet. He sat down, a tired man, and said: "Give me a drink of water." And so, all through His life, it was His simple humanness and love that led Him to others, and led them to Him and to His great salvation.

JUNE 1.

"That the righteousness of the law might be fulfilled in us" (Rom. viii. 4).

Beloved friends, do you know the mistake some of you are making? Some of you say: "It is not possible for me to be good; no man ever was perfect, and it is no use for me to try." That is the mistake many of you are making. I agree with the first sentence, "No man ever was perfect"; but I don't agree with the second, "There is no use trying." There is a divine righteousness that we may have. I don't mean merely that which pardons your sins--I believe that, too--but I mean far more; I mean that which comes into your soul and unites itself with the fibers of your being; I mean Christ; your life, your purity, making you feel as Christ feels; think as Christ thinks, love as Christ loves, hate as Christ hates, and be "partakers of the divine nature." That is God's righteousness; "that the righteousness of the law might be fulfiled in us," not by us, but in us; not our hands and feet merely, but our very instincts, our very desires, our very nature springing up in harmony with His own. Have you got Him, dear friends? He will come and fulfil all right things in you if to-day you will open your heart.

JUNE 2.

"As ye have therefore received Christ Jesus the Lord so walk ye in Him" (Col. ii. 6).

Here is the very core of spiritual life. It is not a subjective state so much as a life in the heart. Christ for us is the ground of our salvation and the source of our justification; Christ in us of our sanctification. When this becomes real, "Ye are dead"; your own condition, states and resources are no longer counted upon any more than a dead man's, but "your life is hid with Christ in God." It is not even always manifest to you. It is hid and so wrapped up and enfolded in Him that only as you abide in Him does it appear and abide. Nay, "Christ who is your life," must Himself ever maintain it, and be made unto you of God all you need. Therefore, Christian life is not to come to Christ to save you, and then go on and work out your sanctification yourself, but "as ye have received Christ Jesus, the Lord, so to walk in Him," just as dependent and as simply trusting as for your pardon and salvation.

Ah friends, how much it would ease our tasks
For the day that's just begun,
To live our life a step at a time
And our moments one by one.

JUNE 3.

"Ye shall receive the power of the Holy Ghost" (Acts i. 8).

There is power for us if we have the Holy Ghost. God wants us to speak to men so that they will feel it, so that they will never forget it. God means every Christian to be effective, to count in the actual records and results of Christian work. Dear friends, God sent you here to be a power yourself. There is not one of you but is an essential wheel of the machinery, and can accomplish all that God calls you to. I solemnly believe that there is not a thing that God expects of man but that God will give the man power to do. There is not a claim God makes on you or me but God will stand up to, and will give what He commands. I believe when Christ Jesus lived and died and sent down the Holy Ghost, He sent resources for all our need, and that there is no place for failure in Christian life if we will take God's resources. Jesus, the ascended One, and the Holy Ghost, the indwelling energy, life and efficiency of God, are sufficient for all possible emergencies. Do you believe this? If you believe it, let Him into your heart, without reserve and allow Him to control and work through you to-day by His power.

JUNE 4.

"Looking unto Jesus" (Heb. xii. 2).

There must be a constant looking unto Jesus, or, as the German Bible gives it, an off-looking upon Jesus; that is, looking off from the evil, refusing to see it, not letting the mind dwell upon it for a second. We should have mental eyelashes as well as physical ones, which can be used like shields, and let no evil thing in; or, like a stockade camp in the woods, which repels the first assault of the enemy. This is the use of the fringes to our eyes, and so it should be with the soul. Many do not seem to know that they have spiritual eyes. They go through the world as if somebody had cut off their eyelashes, and they stare away on the good and evil alike. The devil comes along with his evil pictures and bids them look. We cannot look upon evil without being defiled. Sometimes, in going down the street, the sight of some of the pictures on the way will cast their filth upon the soul so that we shall feel the need of being bathed in Jesus' blood for hours for cleansing. There has been no consent unto sin, but the sight of it has defiled. There is no help for it but in the resolute, steady, inner view of Christ.

JUNE 5.

"My heart is fixed, O God" (Ps. lvii. 7).

We do not always feel joyful, but we are always to count it joy. This word _reckon_ is one of the keywords of Scripture. It is the same word used about our being dead. We are painfully conscious of something which would gladly return to life. But we are to treat ourselves as dead, and neither fear nor obey the old nature. So we are to reckon the thing that comes a blessing; we are determined to rejoice, to say, "My heart is fixed, Lord; I will sing and give praises." This rejoicing by faith will soon become a habit, and will ever bring speedily the spirit of gladness and the spontaneous overflow of praise.

Then, although the fig tree may wither and no fruit appear in the vines, the labor of the olive fail, and the field yield no increase, the herd be cut off from the stall, and the cattle from the field, yet will we rejoice in the Lord and joy in the God of our salvation.

Though the everlasting mountains
And the earth itself remove,

Naught can change His loving kindness
Or His everlasting love.

JUNE 6.

"He emptied Himself" (Phil. ii. 8, R. V.).

The first step to the righteousness of the kingdom is "poor in spirit." Then the next is a little deeper, "they that mourn." Because now you must get plastic, you must get broken, you must get like the metal in the fire, which the Master can mould; and so, it is not enough to see your unrighteousness, but deeply to feel it, deeply to regret it, deeply to mourn over it, to own it not a little thing that sin has come into your life. And so God leads a soul unto His righteousness. He usually leads it through some testings and trials. This generally comes after conversion. I do not think it necessary for a soul to have deep and great suffering before it is saved. I think He will put it into the fire when He knows it is saved; when it realizes it is accepted; when it is not afraid of the discipline; when it is not the hand of wrath, but the hand of love. Oh, then, God, takes you down and makes you poor in spirit, and makes you mourn until you get to the third step, which is to be meek, broken, yielded, submissive, willing, surrendered, and laid low at His feet, crying: "What wilt Thou have me to do?"

JUNE 7.

"When ye go; ye shall not go empty" (Ex. iii. 21).

When we are really emptied He would have us filled with Himself and the Holy Spirit. It is very precious to be conscious of nothing good in ourselves; but, oh, are we also conscious of His great goodness? We may be ready to admit our own disability, but are we as ready to admit His ability? There are many Christians who can say, "We are not sufficient of ourselves to think anything as of ourselves"; but the number I fear is very small who can say, "Our sufficiency is of God."

Are you sure that He is able to provide every want in you, or do you feel that you must supply it yourself? Are you believing that God does now supply every lack in your heart and your life, so that all stumbling is taken away, and you are endowed with power for His service, as Elisha took the empty vessels and filled them before they were set aside to be used? Our Saviour, at Cana, ordered the water-pots to be filled to the brim. Then the water was made into wine, but not until the vessels were full. God wants His children to have always a full heart.

JUNE 8.

"Bread corn is bruised" (Isa. xxviii. 28).

The farmer does not gather timothy and blue grass, and break it with a heavy machine. But he takes great pains with the wheat. So God takes great pains with those who are to be of much use to Him. There is a nature in them that needs this discipline. Don't wonder if the bread corn is treated with the wise, discriminating care that will fit it for food. He knows the way He is taking, and there is infinite tenderness in the oversight He gives. He is watching the furnace you are in lest the heat should be too intense. He wants it great enough to purify, and then it is withdrawn. He knoweth our frame. He will not let any temptation take us but such as is common to man, and He will with the temptation also make a way to escape, that we may be able to bear it. Do you believe in this disciplining love of the Husbandman, and are you trusting Him with the leading and government of your life? Oh, that you would cease to envy or be disturbed by the people around you! Some day you will be glad for the training and blessing they have brought you.

JUNE 9.

"Ye are the light of the world" (Matt. v. 14).

We are called the lights of the world, light-bearers, reflectors, candle-sticks, lamps. We are to be kindled ourselves, and then we will burn and give light to others. We are the only light the world has. The Lord might come down Himself and give light to the world, but He has chosen differently. He wants to send it through us, and if we don't give it the world will not have it. We should be giving light all the time to our neighbors. God does not put a meteor in the sky to tell us when to shine. We are to be giving light all the time wherever we are, at home, or in the social circle, or in our place in the church. We should feel always we may never have another opportunity for it, and so we should always be burning and shining for Him. Let our lamps be trimmed and burning and full of the oil of the Spirit. Above all, let us be a steady light to the lost ones.

Let me dwell in Timnath Serah,
Where the sun forever shines,

90

Where the night and darkness come not,

And the day no more declines.

JUNE 10.

"Your heavenly Father knoweth ye have need" (Matt. vi. 32).

Christ makes no less of our trust for temporal things than He does for spiritual things. He places a good deal of emphasis upon it. Why? Simply because it is harder to trust God for them. In spiritual matters we can fool ourselves, and think that we are trusting when we are not; but we cannot do so about rent and food, and the needs of our body. They must come or our faith fails. It is easy to say that we trust Him in things that are a long way off, but there can be no trifling about it in things where the faith must bring practical answers. It is easy to have faith for our needs, and to trust Him when the sun is shining. But let some things arise which irritate and rasp and fret us, and we soon find whether we have real trust or not. And so the things of everyday life are tests of our real faith in God, and He often puts us where we have to trust for tangible matters--for money and rent, and food and clothes. If you are not trusting here wholly, when you are placed in such tests you will break down. Are you trusting God for everything through the six ordinary days of the week?

JUNE 11.

"Thou hast the dew of thy youth" (Ps. cx. 3).

Oh, that you might get such a view of Him as would make it impossible for little things ever to fret you again! The petty cares and silly trifles that have troubled you so much ought rather to fill you with wonder that you can think so much about them. Oh, if you had the dew of His youth you should go forth as the morning and fulfil the promise of a glorious day! What a difference it has made in life since we have seen it was possible to do this! How easy it seems now when the little troubles come, to draw a little closer to Christ, to drink in a little more of that fountain of life, to get a little nearer to that loving heart, and to draw in great draughts of refreshing and strength from it. How clear it makes the brain for work! Coming to Him thus, heavy and dull and tired, how rested you become and able to spring forth ready for work. How inspiring to think that our living Head never grows weary. He is as fresh as He ever was; He is a glorious conqueror; He is ever the victorious Christ. Let Him take you to-day, and He will cause you to see in Him the invincible Leader!

JUNE 12.

"We would see Jesus" (John xii. 21).

Glory to Him for all the things laid up for us in the days to come. Glory to Him for all the visions of service in the future; the opportunities of doing good that are far away as well as close at hand. Our Saviour was able to despise the cross for the joy that was before Him. Let us look up to Him, and rise up to Him till we get on high and are able to look out from the mount of vision over all the land of far distances. There shall not a single thing come to us in all the future in which we may not be able to see the King in His beauty. Let us be very sure that we do not see anything else. Our pupils will become impressed as they look at this vision, so that they will not be able to reflect anything else. My little child came to me once and said: "Papa, look at that golden sign across the street a good while; now look at that brick wall and tell me what you see." "Why, I see the golden sign on the brick wall." And he laughed merrily over it. So, if we look a long time upon Jesus we cannot look at anything else without seeing a reflection of Him. Everything which we behold will become a part of Him.

JUNE 13.

"The sweetness of the lips increaseth learning" (Prov. xvi. 21).

Life is very largely made up of words. They are not so emphatic, perhaps, as deeds. Deeds are more deliberate expressions of thought. One of the most remarkable authors of the New Testament has said, "If any man offend not in word, the same is a perfect man." It is very often a test of victory in Christian life. Our triumph in this often depends on what we say, or what we do not say. It is said by James of the tongue, "It is set on fire of hell." The true Christian, therefore, is righteous in his ways and upright in his words. His deeds appeal to men; but in speech he is looking up, for God is listening. His words are sent upward and recorded for the judgment. I believe that this is an actual fact, and I can almost fancy that the skies above, which seem so transparent, the beautiful blue ether over our heads, is like a waxen tablet with a finely sensitive surface, and receives an impression of every word we speak, and that then these tablets are hardened and preserved for the eternal judgment. So we should speak, dear

92

friends, with our eyes ever upward, never forgetting that we shall some day meet the words that we have spoken.

JUNE 14.

"The secret of the Lord is with them that fear Him" (Ps. xxv. 14).

There are secrets of Providence which God's dear children may learn. His dealing with them often seems, to the outward eye, dark and terrible. Faith looks deeper and says, "This is God's secret. You look only on the outside; I can look deeper and see the hidden meaning." Sometimes diamonds are done up in rough packages, so that their value cannot be seen. When the tabernacle was built in the wilderness there was nothing rich in its outside appearance. The costly things were all within, and its outward covering of rough badger skin gave no hint of the valuable things which it contained. God may send you, dear friends, some costly packages. Do not worry if they are done up in rough wrappings. You may be sure there are treasures of love, and kindness and wisdom hidden within. Do not be so foolish as to throw away a nugget of gold because there is some quartz in it. If we take what He sends, and trust Him for the goodness in it, even in the dark, we shall learn the meaning of the secrets of His providence.

JUNE 15.

"Grow up into Him in all things" (Eph. iv. 15).

Harvest is a time of ripeness. Then the fruit and grain are fully developed, both in size and weight. Time has tempered the acid of the green fruit. It has been mellowed and softened by the rains and the heat of summer. The sun has tinted it into rich colors, and at last it is ready and ripe to fall into the hand. So Christian life ought to be. There are many things in life that need to be mellowed and ripened. Many Christians have orchards full of fruit, but they are all green and sharp to the taste. There is a great deal in them that is good, but it is incomplete, and very sharp and sour. Perhaps something goes wrong in your domestic life, and you get flurried and cross and lose your confidence in God, and then, of course, your Christian joy. These things produce regret and all kinds of misery. There are many things day after day you are sorry for. You know you are not ripe and mellow and you cannot become so by trying. You cannot bring the sweetness in. It must be wrought out from within.

JUNE 16.

"Ye cannot serve God and Mammon" (Matt. vi. 24).

He does not say ye cannot very well serve God and mammon, but ye cannot serve two masters at all. Ye shall be sure to end by serving one. The man who thinks he is serving God a little is deceived; he is not serving God. God will not have his service. The devil will monopolize him before he gets through. A divided heart loses both worlds. Saul tried it. Balaam tried it. Judas tried it, and they all made a desperate failure. Mary had but one choice. Paul said: "This one thing I do." "For me to live is Christ." Of such a life God says: "Because he hath set his love upon Me therefore will I deliver him. I will set him on high because he hath known My name." God takes a peculiar pride in showing His love to the heart that wholly chooses Him. Heaven and earth will fade away before its trust can be disappointed. Have we chosen Him only and given Him all our heart?

Say is it all for Jesus,

As you so often sing?

Is He your Royal Master?

Is He your heart's dear King?

JUNE 17.

"The glory of the Lord shall be thy reward" (Isa. lviii. 8).

He comes by our side as our helper; nay, more. He comes to dwell within us; to be the life in our blood, the fire in our thought, the faith within us, both in inception and consummation. Thus He becomes not only the recompense of the victor, but the resources of the victory. He is the Captain and the Overcomer in our lives. If we have caught any help that has relieved us of a troubled morning, it has been of Him. He lifts our eyes up unto Himself and delivers us from apathy, from discontent and from fears. He is always the helper in this heavenly competition, and will be the great reward in all the ages to come. If our life is hidden with Him we shall have to go through the same trials that He went through, but we shall not find them too hard. If once we take Him fully as the strength of our life, and our all in all, we shall be able to lay aside all the hindering things that press upon us day by day.

I have overcome, overcome,

Overcome for thee,

.

94

Thou shalt overcome, overcome,

Overcome thro' Me.

JUNE 18.

"I am doing a great work, so that I cannot come down" (Neh. vi. 3).

When work is pressing there are many little things that will come and seem to need attention. Then it is a very blessed thing to be quiet and still, and work on, and trust the little things with God. He answers such trust in a wonderful way. If the soul has no time to fret and worry and harbor care, it has learned the secret of faith in God. A desperate desire to get some difficulty right takes the eye off of God and His glory. Some dear ones have been so anxious to get well, and have spent so much time in trying to claim it, that they have lost their spiritual blessing. God sometimes has to teach such souls that there must be a willingness to be sick before they are so thoroughly yielded as to receive His fullest blessing.

The enemy often keeps at this work. Sanballat came four times to Nehemiah and received always the same answer. It is best to stick to a good answer. How many fears we have stopped to fight which have proved to be nothing at last. Nehemiah recognized that fear was sin, and did not dare to yield to it.

JUNE 19.

"Who hath first given to Him, and it shall be recompensed unto him again" (Rom. xi. 35).

The Christian women of the world have it in their power, by a very little sacrifice, to add millions to the treasury of the Lord. Beloved sisters, have you found the joy of sacrifice for Jesus? Have you given up something that you might give it to Him? Are you giving your substance to Jesus? He will take it, and He will give you a thousandfold more. I should rather be connected with a work founded on great sacrifice than on enormous endowments. The reason God loved the place where His ancient temple rose in majesty was because there Abraham offered his son and David his treasure. The reason redemption is so dear to the Father and the heavenly world is because its foundation-stone is the Cross of Calvary. And the Christian life that is dearest to the heart of God, and will rise to the highest glory and usefulness, is the one whose foundation principle is sacrifice and self-renunciation. This is why the Master teaches us to give, because giving means loving, and love is but another name for life.

JUNE 20.

"Let every man abide in the same calling wherein he was called" (I. Cor. vii. 20).

O ye who complain about your calling or fret about the changes and trials of life, how do you know but that these very changes are the divine methods by which God's purposes of blessing and usefulness concerning you be fulfilled? Had Aquila not been compelled to leave Rome and break up his home and business, he would probably have never met with Paul, and been called to the knowledge and service of Christ through this providential meeting. Had he not been a working man, and pursuing his ordinary avocation he would not have been brought into contact with the apostle. It was in the line of their calling, their common duties, and the providential changes of their life that God called them. And so He meets us. Do not try hard to run away from it, but, as the apostle has so finely put it, "Let every man abide in the same calling wherein he is called, let him therein abide with God." Make the most of your incidental opportunities.

JUNE 21.

"God hath set some in the church ... helps" (I. Cor. xii. 28).

In the apostle's lists of officers in the church the "helps" are mentioned before the "governments." By the ministry of prayer, by the ministry of giving, by the ministry of encouragement, by the shining face and mute pressure of the hand, and a little word of cheer, and by the countless ways in which we can help, or at least can keep from hindering, we can all find still the footprints of Aquila and Priscilla, if we want to follow them. It is a great grace to be able to rejoice in another's work and pour our lives, like affluent rivers, into great streams. But God knows whence every drop has come, and in the greater day of recompense many of the helps shall have the chief reward. Beloved, are you helping? Are you helping your pastor, your brother, your husband, your mother, your fellow-worker, and when the harvest comes shall he that soweth and he that reapeth rejoice together?

You can help by holy prayer,
Helpful love and joyful song,
O, the burdens you may bear,
O, the sorrows you may share,

O, the crowns you yet may wear,

If you help along.

JUNE 22.

"This is that bread which came down from heaven" (John vi. 58).

We had the sentence of death in ourselves that we should not trust in ourselves, but in God which raiseth the dead; who delivereth us from so great a death, who doth deliver; in whom we trust that He will yet deliver us. This was the supernatural secret of Paul's life; he drew continually in his body from the strength of Christ, his Risen Head. The body which rose from Joseph's tomb was to him a physical reality and the inexhaustible fountain of his vital forces. More than any other he has imparted to us the secret of His strength; "We are members of His body, of His flesh and of His bones"; "The Lord is for the body and the body is for the Lord." Marvelous truth! Divine Elixir of Life and Fountain of Perpetual Youth! Earnest of the Resurrection! Fulfilment of the ancient psalms and songs of faith! "The Lord is the strength of my life, of whom shall I be afraid? My flesh and my heart faint and fail, but God is the strength of my heart and my portion forever." Beloved, have we learned this secret, and are we living the life of the Incarnate One in our flesh?

JUNE 23.

"Now we are the sons of God, and it doth not yet appear what we shall be" (I. John iii. 2).

We are the sons of God. We are not merely called and even legally declared, but actually are sons of God by receiving the life and nature of God; and so we are the very brethren of our Lord; not only in His human nature, but still more in His divine relationship. "Therefore, He is not ashamed to call us brethren." He gives us that which entitles us to that right, and makes us worthy of it. He does not introduce us into a position for which we are uneducated and unfitted, but He gives us a nature worthy of our glorious standing; and as He shall look upon us in our complete and glorious exaltation reflecting His own likeness and shining in His Father's glory, He shall have no cause to be ashamed of us. Even now He is pleased to acknowledge us before the universe and call us brethren in the sight of all earth and heaven. Oh, how this dignifies the humblest saint of God! How little we need mind the misunderstanding of the world if He "is not ashamed to call us brethren."

So let us go out to-day to represent His royal family.

JUNE 24.

"I will clothe thee with change of raiment" (Zech. iii. 4).

For Paul every exercise of the Christian life was simply the grace of Jesus Christ imparted to him and lived out by him, so that holiness was to put on the Lord Jesus and all the robes of His perfect righteousness which he loves to describe so often in his beautiful epistles. "Put on therefore, as the elect of God, holy and beloved," he says to the Colossians, "bowels of mercies, kindness, humbleness of mind, meekness, long suffering"; and, "above all these things, put on love which is the bond of perfectness." None of these things are regarded as intrinsic qualities in us, but as imparted graces from the hand of Jesus. And even in the later years of his life, and after the mature experience of a quarter of a century we find him exclaiming, "I count all things but loss for the excellency of the knowledge of Christ Jesus, my Lord; for whom I have suffered the loss of all things, and count them but refuse, that I might win Christ and be found in Him."

Lord, enable us to-day to go out, clothed in Thy robes of perfect rightness and with our hearts in adjustment with Thy perfect love.

JUNE 25.

"Who leadeth us in triumph" (II. Cor. ii. 14).

Every victor must first be a self-conqueror. But the method of Joshua's victory was the uplifted arm of Moses on the Mount. As he held up his hands Joshua prevailed, as he lowered them Amalek prevailed. It was to be a battle of faith and not of human strength, and the banner that was to wave over the discomfited foe, "Jehovah-nissi." This, too, is the secret of our spiritual triumph. "If we are led of the Spirit we shall not fulfil the lusts of the flesh." "Sin shall not have dominion over you, for ye are not under the law but under grace."

Have we thus begun the battle and in the strength of Christ planted our feet on our own necks, and thus victorious over the enemy in the citadel of the heart been set at liberty for the battle of the Lord and the service of others? It was the lack of this that hindered the life of Saul and it has wrecked many a promising career. One enemy in the heart is stronger than ten thousand in the field. May the Lord lead us all into Joshua's first triumph, and show us the secret of self-crucifixion through the greater Joshua, who alone can lead us on to holiness and victory!

JUNE 26.

"When He saw the multitudes He was moved" (Matt. ix. 36).

He is able to be "touched with the feeling of our infirmities." The word "touched" expresses a great deal. It means that our troubles are His troubles, and that in all our afflictions He is afflicted. It is not a sympathy of sentiment, but a sympathy of suffering.

There is much help in this for the tired heart. It is the foundation of His Priesthood, and God meant that it should be to us a source of unceasing consolation. Let us realize, more fully, our oneness with our Great High Priest, and cast all our burdens on His great heart of love. If we know what it is to ache in every nerve with the responsive pain of our suffering child, we can form some idea of how our sorrows touch His heart, and thrill His exalted frame. As the mother feels her babe's pain, as the heart of friendship echoes every cry from another's woe, so in heaven, our exalted Saviour, even amid the raptures of that happy world, is suffering in His Spirit and even in His flesh with all His children bear. "Seeing then we have such a great high Priest, let us come boldly to the throne of grace," and let us come to our great High Priest.

JUNE 27.

"Be filled with the Spirit" (Eph. v. 18).

Some of the effects of being filled with the Spirit are:

1. Holiness of heart and life. This is not the perfection of the human nature, but the holiness of the divine nature dwelling within.
2. Fulness of joy so that the heart is constantly radiant. This does not depend on circumstances, but fills the spirit with holy laughter in the midst of the most trying surroundings.
3. Fulness of wisdom, light and knowledge, causing us to see things as He sees them.
4. An elevation, improvement and quickening of the mind by an ability to receive the fulfilment of the promise, "We have the mind of Christ."
5. An equal quickening of the physical life. The body was made for the Holy Ghost, as well as the mind and soul.
6. An ability to pray the prayer of the Holy Ghost. If He is in us there will be a strange accordance with God's working in the world around us. There is a divine harmony between the Spirit and Providence.

JUNE 28.

"Leaning upon her beloved" (Songs of Solomon viii. 5).

Shall you make the claim most practical and real and lean like John your full weight on the Lord's breast? That is the way He would have us prove our love. "If you love me lean hard," said a heathen woman to her missionary, as she was timidly leaning her tired body upon her stalwart breast. She felt slighted by the timorous reserve, and asked the confidence that would lay all its weight upon the one she trusted. And He says to us, "Casting all your care upon Him for He careth for you." He would have us prove our love by a perfect trust that makes no reserve. He is able to carry all our care, to manage all our interests, to satisfy all our needs. Let us go forth leaning on His breast and feeding on His life. For John not only leaned but also fed. It was at supper that he leaned. This is the secret of feeding on Him, to rest upon His bosom. This is the need of the fevered heart of man. Let us cry to Him, "Tell me whom my soul loveth, where thou feedest, where thou makest thy flock to rest at noon."

JUNE 29.

"He dwelleth with you and shall be in you" (John xiv. 17).

Do not fail to mark these two stages in Christian life. The one is the Spirit's work in us, the other is the Spirit's personal coming to abide within us. All true Christians know the first, but few, it is to be feared, understand and receive the second. There is a great difference between my building a house and my going to reside in that house and make it my home. And there is a great difference between the Holy Spirit's work in regenerating a soul--the building of a house, and His coming to reside, abide and control in our innermost spirit and our whole life and being.

Have we received Him Himself not as our Guest, but as the Owner, Proprietor and Keeper of the temple He has built to be "an habitation of God through the Spirit"?

This is my wonderful story,

Christ to my heart has come,

Jesus the King of glory,

Finds in my heart a home.

I am so glad I received Him,

Jesus, my heart's dear King,

I, who so often have grieved Him,

All to His feet would bring.

JUNE 30.

"Therefore, choose" (Deut. xxx. 19).

Men are choosing every day the spiritual or earthly. And as we choose we are taking our place unconsciously with the friends of Christ, or the world. It is not merely what ye say, it is what we prefer.

When Solomon made his great choice at Gibeon, God said to him, "Because this was in thine heart to ask wisdom, therefore will I give it unto thee, and all else besides that thou didst not choose." It was not merely that he said it because it was right to say, and would please God if he said it. But it was the thing his heart preferred, and God saw it in his heart and gave it to him with all besides that he had not chosen. What are we choosing, beloved? It is our choice that settles our destiny. It is not how we feel, but how we purpose. Have we chosen the good part? Have we said, "Whatever else I am or have, let me be God's child, let me have His favor and blessing, let me please Him?" Or have we said, "I must have this thing, and then I will see about religion." Alas, God has seen what was in thine heart, and perhaps He has already said, "They have their reward."

JULY 1.

"After that ye have suffered awhile" (I. Peter v. 10).

Beloved, are we learning love in the school of suffering? Are our hearts being mellowed and deepened by the summer heat of trial until the fruit of the Spirit, "which is love, joy, peace, long-suffering, gentleness, meekness, temperance, faith, is ripening for the harvest of His coming, and our sufferings are easily borne for His sake"? Oh, this is the school of love, and makes Him unutterably more dear to our hearts and us to His. And thus only can we ever learn with Him the heavenly charity which "suffers long, and is kind."

We see the very first and the very last feature of the face of love, as delineated in St. Paul's portrait (I. Cor. xiii.), are marks of pain and patient suffering, "suffers long," "endureth all things." So let us learn thus in the school of love to suffer and be kind, to endure all things.

Surely it will not be hard to love through all when it is the heart of Jesus within us which will love and continue to love to the very end.

101

I want the love that suffers and is kind,

That envies not nor vaunts its pride or fame,

Is not puffed up, does no discourteous act,

Is not provoked, nor seeks its own to claim.

JULY 2.

"And hath raised us up together" (Eph. ii. 6).

Ascension is more than resurrection. Much is said of it in the New Testament. Christ riseth above all things. We see Him in the very act of ascending as we do not in the actual resurrection, as, with hands and lips engaged in blessing, He gently parts from their side, so simply, so unostentatiously, with so little imposing ceremony as to make heaven so near to our common life that we can just whisper through. And we, too, must ascend, even here. "If ye then be risen with Christ, seek those things that are above." We must learn to live on the heaven side and look at things from above. How it overcomes sin, defies Satan, dissolves perplexities, lifts us above trials, separates us from the world and conquers the fear of death to contemplate all things as God sees them, as Christ beholds them, as we shall one day look back upon them from His glory, and as if we were now really "Seated with Him," as indeed we are, "in the heavenly places." Let us arise with His resurrection and in fellowship with His glorious ascension learn henceforth to live above.

JULY 3.

"Look from the top" (Song of Solomon iv. 8).

Yes, our perplexities would become plain if we kept on a spiritual elevation. How often when the traveler quite loses his way he can soon find it again from some tree top or some hill top where all the winding paths he has gone spread behind him, and the whole homeward road opens before. So, from the heights of prayer and faith, we too can see the plain path, and know that we are going home.

There is no other way in which we can gain the victory over the world. We must get above it. We must see it from the side of our great reward. Then it looks like earthly objects after we have gazed upon the sun for a while. We are blind to them. When the Italian fruit-seller finds that he is heir to a ducal palace you cannot tempt him any more with the paltry profits of his trade or the company of his old associates. He is above it all. They who know the hope of their calling and

102

the riches of the glory of their inheritance can well despise the world. It is the poor starving ones who go hungering for the husks of earth. We are born from above and have a longing to go home. Let us go forth to-day with our hearts on the homestretch.

JULY 4.

"Whosoever abideth in Him sinneth not" (I. John iii. 6).

In sanctification what becomes of the old nature? Many people are somewhat unduly concerned to know if it can be killed outright, and seem to desire a sort of certificate of its death and burial. It is enough to know that it is without and Christ is within. It may show itself again, and even knock at the door and plead for admittance, but it is forever outside while we abide in Him. Should we step out of Him and into sin we might find the old corpse in the ghastly cemetery, and its foul aroma might yet revive and embrace us once more. But he that abideth in Him sinneth not and cannot sin while he so abides.

Therefore let us abide and let us not be anxious to escape the hold of eternal vigilance and ceaseless abiding. Our paths are made and the strength to pursue them; let us walk in them. God has provided for us a full sanctification. Is it strange that He should demand it of us, and require us to be holy, even as He is holy, seeing He has given us His own holiness. So let us put on our beautiful garments and prepare to walk in white with Him.

JULY 5.

"A garden enclosed" (Song of Solomon iv. 12).

The figure here is a garden enclosed, not a wilderness. The garden soil is a cultivated soil, very different from the roadside or the wilderness. The idea of a garden is culture. The ground has to be prepared, to be broken up by ploughing, to be mellowed by harrowing, all the stones removed, the roots of all natural growth dug up, for the good things we are seeking are not natural growths and will not grow in our soil. We all start on the old basis and try to improve the old nature, but that is not God's way. His way is to get self out of the way entirely, and let Him create anew out of nothing, so that all shall be of Him; and we must find Jesus the Alpha and Omega.

103

The thing you want to learn here is to die. There can be no real life till self dies, and don't try to die yourself, but ask God to slay you, and He will make a thorough work of it.

This the secret nature hideth,

Summer dies and lives again,

Spring from winter's grave ariseth,

Harvest grows from buried grain.

JULY 6.

"I am my beloved's" (Song of Solomon vii. 10).

If you want power you must compress. It is the shutting in of the steam that moves the engine. The amount of powder on a flat surface that sends a ball to its destination when shut up in a gun only makes a flash. If you want to carry the electric current you must be insulated. Stand a man on a glass platform and turn a battery on him and he will be filled with electricity. Let him step off the glass, and the moment he touches earth he loses power.

We must be inclosed by His everlasting Covenant. That holds us and keeps us from falling. He will be a wall of fire round about us. He comes Himself and envelops us round about with the old Shekinah glory, and will be the glory in the midst. He wants us inclosed--by a distinct act of consecration dedicated wholly to Him. Are you inclosed by His fences, His commandments, His promises, His covenant? Is your heart really and only for the Lord?

If not, come to Him now and let Him separate you from all the things that take your life, and let Him separate you unto Himself, the Life Giver.

JULY 7.

"And the glory of the Lord filled the tabernacle" (Ex. xl. 35).

In the last chapter of Exodus we read all the Lord commanded Moses to do, and that as he fulfilled these commands the glory of the Lord descended and filled the tabernacle till there was no room for Moses, and from that time the pillar of cloud overshadowed them, their guide, their protection. And so we have been building as the Lord Himself commanded, and now the temple is to be handed over to Him to be possessed and filled. He will so fill you, if you will let Him that yourself and everything else will be taken out of the way, the glory of the Lord will fill the temple, encompassing, lifting up, guiding, keeping; and from this time your moon shall not withdraw its light, nor your sun go down.

Do you want power? You have God for it. Do you want holiness? You have God for it; and so of everything. And God is bending down from His throne to-day to lift you up to your true place in Him. From this time may the cloud of His glory so surround and fill us that we shall be lost sight of forever.

JULY 8.

"Having begun in the Spirit, are ye now made perfect by the flesh" (Gal. iii. 3).

Grace literally means that which we do not have to earn. It has two great senses always; it comes for nothing and it comes when we are helpless; it doesn't merely help the man that helps himself--that is not the Gospel; the Gospel is that God helps the man who can't help himself. And then there is another thing; God helps the man to help himself, for everything the man does comes from God. Grace is given to the man who is so weak and helpless he cannot take the first step. That is the meaning of grace--a little of the meaning of it; we can never know the fulness it has. Now, this river is as free as it is full, but you know some people have an idea when they get a little farther on they have got to pay an admission, and reserved seats are very high, and they shrink back from the higher blessings of the Gospel; ordinary Christians scarcely dare to claim them. If I understand the meaning of this, God has not put the higher blessings apart for a separate class who somehow are nearer to Him. God is no respecter of persons.

JULY 9.

"Cast thy burden on the Lord" (Ps. lv. 22).

Dear friends, sometimes we bring a burden to God, and we have such a groaning over it, and we seem to think God has a dreadful time, too, but in reality it does not burden Him at all. God says: It is a light thing for Me to do this for you. Your load, though heavy for you, is not heavy for Him. Christ carries the whole on one shoulder, not two shoulders. The government of the world is upon His shoulder. He is not struggling and groaning with it. His mighty arm is able to carry all your burdens. There is power in Christ for our sanctification. He is able to sanctify you. Yes, yes, the Lord can sanctify, the Lord can heal, the Lord can do anything. You must have faith in God. If you come to this river this morning, it will take you as your Niagara would take a little boat, and just bear you down--to a precipice? Oh, no, but to the bosom of love and blessing forever.

Oft there comes a wondrous message,

When my hopes are growing dim,

I can hear it thro' the darkness

Like some sweet and far-off hymn.

Nothing is too hard for Jesus,

No man can work like Him.

JULY 10.

"That we might know the things that are freely given to us of God" (I. Cor. ii. 12).

The highest blessings of the Gospel are just as free as the lowest; and when you have served Him ten years you cannot sit down and say, "I have got an experience now and I count on that." How often we do that; we say, "Now I know I am saved, I feel it." And so we are building a different foundation--we are building on something in ourselves. Always take grace as something you don't deserve, something that is freely bestowed. The long, deep, boundless river is free; it is as free at the mouth as it is at the little stream, and free all the way along, and anybody can come and drink, and anybody can come and bathe in its boundless waters. Are you going to believe it?

God has given us His Holy Spirit that we may "know the things that are freely given of us of God." It is a hard thing for the poor child to look in through the window and see a fire, and the happy family sitting around the table when it is starving. What is the good of knowing that there is warmth, and love, and light, if it is not free? God has freely given all the goodness of His grace and love.

JULY 11.

"For it is God which worketh in you" (Phil. ii. 13).

A day with Jesus. Let us seek its plan and direction from Him. Let us take His highest thought and will for us in it. Let us look to Him for our desires, ideals, expectations in it. Then shall it bring to us exceeding abundantly above all that we can ask or think. Let Him be our Guide and Way. Let us not so much be thinking even of His plan and way as of Him as the Personal Guide of every moment, on whom we constantly depend to lead our every step.

106

Let Him also be the sufficiency and strength of all the day. Let us never forget the secret: "I can do all things through Christ who strengtheneth me." Let us have Jesus Christ Himself in us to do the works, and let us every moment fall back on Him, both to will and do in us of His good pleasure. Let our holiness be "the law of the spirit of life in Christ Jesus." Let our health be the "life of Jesus manifest in our mortal flesh." Let our faith be "the faith of the Son of God who loved us." Let our peace and joy be His peace and joy. And let our service be not our works, but the grace of Christ within us.

JULY 12.

"When ye pray, believe that ye receive" (Mark xi. 24).

Consecration is entered by an act of faith. You are to take the gift from God, believe you have, and confess that you have it. Step out on it firmly, and let the devil know you have it as well as the Lord. When once you say to Him boldly, "I am Thine," He answers back from the heavenly heights, "Thou art Mine," and the echoes go ringing down through all your life, "Mine! Thine!" If you dare confess Christ as your Saviour and Sanctifier He has bound Himself to make it a reality, but you must stand behind His mighty Word. It is the essence of testimony to tell of what Jesus has promised to become to you. It is right to have glorious words of thanksgiving, but these are not exactly testimony. God would have us put our seal on the promises, and lift up our hands and acknowledge them as ours.

Then you are to ignore the old life and reckon it no longer yours if it should come up again. Every time it appears say, "This is from the under world. I am sitting in the heavenly places with Christ."

JULY 13.

"Even Christ pleased not Himself" (Rom. xv. 3).

Let this be a day of self-forgetting ministry for Christ and others. Let us not once think of being ministered unto, but say ever with Him: "I am among you as He that doth serve." Let us not drag our burdens through the day, but drop all our loads of care and be free to carry His yoke and His burden. Let us make the happy exchange, giving ours and taking His. Let the covenant be: "Thou shalt abide for Me, I also for thee." So shall we lose our heaviest load--ourselves--and so shall we find our highest joy, divine love, the more blessed "to give" than "to receive." Let us do good to all men as we have opportunity. Let us lose no opportunity of blessing, and let us study ingenious ways of service and usefulness. Especially let us seek to win souls.

The Days of Heaven are busy days,

They serve continually,

So spent for Thee and Thine, our days,

As the Days of Heaven would be.

The Days of Heaven are loving days,

As one they all agree,

So linked in loving unity

May our days as Heaven be.

JULY 14.

"Men ought always to pray" (Luke xviii. 1).

Let this be a day of prayer. Let us see that our highest ministry and power is to deal with God for men. Let us be obedient to all the Holy Spirit's voices of prayer in us. Let us count every pressure a call to prayer. Let us cherish the spirit of unceasing prayer and abiding communion. Let us learn the meaning of the ministry of prayer. Let us reach persons this day we cannot reach in person; let us expect results that we have never dared to claim before; let us count every difficulty only a greater occasion for prayer, and let us call on God, who will show us many great and mighty things which we know not.

And let it be a day of joy and praise. Let us live in the promises of God and the outlook of His deliverance and blessing. Let us never dwell on the trial but always on the victory just before. Let us not dwell in the tomb, but in the garden of Joseph and the light of the resurrection. Let us keep our faces toward the sun rising. Arise, shine. Rejoice evermore. In everything give thanks. Praise ye the Lord.

Lord, give us Thy joy in our hearts which shall lift us to lift others, and fill us so we may overflow to others.

JULY 15.

"I am my Beloved's and my Beloved is mine" (Song of Solomon vi. 3).

If I am the Lord's then the Lord is mine. If Christ owns me I own Him. And so faith must reach out and claim its full inheritance and begin to use its great resources. Moment by moment we may now take Him as our grace and strength, our faith and love, our victory and joy, our all in all. And as we thus claim Him we will find His grace sufficient for us, and begin to learn that giving all is just receiving all. Yes, consecration is getting Him fully instead of our own miserable life. There are, indeed, two sides of it. There are two persons in the consecration. One of them is the dear Lord Himself. "And for their sakes," He says, "I consecrate Myself that they also might be consecrated through the truth." The moment we consecrate ourselves to Him He consecrates Himself to us, and henceforth, the whole strength of His life and love and everlasting power is dedicated to keep and complete our consecration, and to make the very best and most of our consecrated life. Who would not give himself to such a Saviour? Surely we will to-day, first give ourselves and then give Him each moment as it comes, to be filled and used.

JULY 16.

"As the hart panteth after the waterbrooks, so panteth my soul after Thee, O God" (Ps. xlii. 1).

First in order to a consecrated life there must be a sense of need, the need of purity, of power, and of a greater nearness to the Lord. There often comes in Christian life a second conviction. It is not now a sense of guilt and God's wrath so much as of the power and evil of inward sin, and the unsatisfactoriness of the life the soul is living. It usually comes from the deeper revelation of God's truth, from more spiritual teaching, from definite examples and testimonies of this life in others, and often from an experience of deep trial, conflict and temptation in which the soul has found its attainments and resources inadequate for the real issues and needs of life. The first result is often a deep discouragement and even despair, but the valley of Achor is the door of hope, and the seventh chapter of Romans with its bitter cry, "O wretched man that I am," is the gateway to the eighth with its shout of triumph, "The Spirit of life in Christ hath made me free from the law of sin and death."

JULY 17.

"By one offering He hath perfected forever them that are sanctified" (Heb. x. 14).

Are you missing what belongs to you? He has promised to sanctify you. He has promised sanctification for you by coming to you Himself and being made of

God to you sanctification. Jesus is my sanctification. Having Him I have obedience, rest, patience and everything I need. He is alive forevermore. If you have Him nothing can be against you. Your temptations will not be against you; your bad temper will not be against you; your hard life, your circumstances, even the devil himself will not be against you. Every time he comes to attack you, he will only root you deeper in Christ. You will become a coward at the thought of being alone; you will be thrown on Jesus every time a trouble assails you. All things henceforth will work together for good to your own soul. Since God is for you nothing can be against you.

My heavenly Bridegroom sought me and called me one glad day, "Arise, my love, my fair one, arise and come away,"
I listened to His pleading, I gave Him all my heart,
And we are one forever and nevermore shall part.

JULY 18.

"Ye are complete in Him" (Col. ii. 10).

In Him we are now complete. The perfect pattern of the life of holy service for which He has redeemed and called us, is now in Him in heaven, even as the architect's model is planned and prepared and completed in his office. But now it must be wrought into us and transferred to our earthly life, and this is the Holy Spirit's work. He takes the gifts and graces of Christ and brings them into our life, as we need and receive them day by day, just as the sections of the vessel are reproduced in the distant Continent, and thus we receive of His fulness, even grace for grace, His grace for our grace, His supply for our need, His strength for our strength, His body for our body, His Spirit for our spirit, and He just "made unto us of God wisdom, righteousness, sanctification and redemption."

But it is much more than mere abstract help and grace, much more even than the Holy Spirit bringing us strength, and peace, and purity. It is personal companionship with Jesus Himself!

Lord, help us receive from Thee to-day, that grace in all trial that shall mean our perfecting in Thee.

JULY 19.

"Nevertheless, David took the castle of Zion" (I. Chron. xi. 5).

110

Many of you have so much fighting to do because you do not have one sharp, decisive battle to begin with. It is far easier to have one great battle than to keep on skirmishing all your life. I know men who spend forty years fighting what they call their besetting sin, and on which they waste strength enough to evangelize the world.

Dear friends, does it pay to throw away your lives? Have one battle, one victory and then praise God. So they had rest from their enemies round about. There is labor to enter in. The height is steep. The way of the cross is not an easy way. It is hard to enter in, but having entered in there is perfect rest. May God help us and give us His perfect rest.

O come and leave thy sinful self forever
Beneath the fountain of the Saviour's blood;
O come, and take Him as thy Sanctifier,
Come thou with us and we will do thee good.

Come to the land where all the foes are vanquished,
And sorrow, sin, disease and death subdued;
O weary soul! by Satan bruised and baffled,
Come thou with us and we will do thee good.

JULY 20.

"Forget also thine own" (Ps. xlv. 10).

We, too, like the ancient Levites, must be "consecrated every one upon our son and upon our brother," and "forget our kindred and our father's house" in every sense in which they could hinder our full liberty and service for the Lord. We, too, must let our business go if it stands between us and the Lord, and in any case let it henceforth be His business and His alone, pursued for Him, controlled by Him, and its profits wholly dedicated to Him, and used as He shall direct. And, like James and John, you must be willing to give up "the hired servants" too. It will make a great difference in your way of living. It will be a change to give up your ease and luxury, your being waited upon and indulged in every wish, and have to do your own work, to give up the attentions of others, to put with privations, and inconveniences, and humiliations, but it will be easy to do it with Him. He never owned a foot of land. He never rode in a carriage. He never had a hired servant. He lay down at last in a borrowed grave. But He is rich enough now, and so will you be some day if you can only be willing to suffer and to wait.

JULY 21.

"Look from the place where thou art" (Gen. xiii. 14).

Let us now see the blessedness of faith. Our own littleness and nothingness sometimes becomes bondage. We are so small in our own eyes we dare not claim God's mighty promises. We say: "If I could be sure I was in God's way I could trust." This is all wrong. Self-consciousness is a great barrier to faith. Get your eyes on Him and Him alone; not on your faith, but on the Author of your faith; not a half look, but a steadfast, prolonged look, with a true heart and fixedness of purpose, that knows no faltering, no parleying with the enemy without a shadow of fear. When you get afraid you are almost sure to fail.

Travelers who have crossed the Alps know how dangerous those mountain passes are, how narrow the foothold, how deep the rocky ravines and how necessary to safety it is that you should look up continually; one downward glance into the dizzy depths would be fatal; and so if we would surmount the heights of faith we must look up--look up. Get your eyes off yourself, off surrounding circumstances, off means, off gifts, to the Great Giver.

JULY 22.

"He that ministereth let us wait on our ministering" (Rom. xii. 7).

Beloved, are you ministering to Christ? Are you doing it with your hands? Are you doing it with your substance and with what you have? Is He getting the best of what is most real to you? Has He a place at your table? And when He does not come to fill the chair, is it free to His representative, His poor and humble children? Your words and wishes are cheap if they do not find expression in your actual gifts. Even Mary did not put Him off with the incense of her heart, but laid her costliest gifts at His feet.

Ye busy women, who work so hard to dress your children and furnish your houses and tables, what have your hands earned for the Master, what have you done or sacrificed for Jesus? "Can you afford it?" was asked of a noble woman, as she promised a costly offering for the Master's work. "No," was her noble reply, "but I can sacrifice it." Let us to-day look around us and see, what we do and give more to the loving Saviour, who gave up His whole life for us.

JULY 23.

"Bring them hither to Me" (Matt. xiv. 18).

Why have ye not received all the fulness of the Holy Spirit? And how may we be anointed with "the rest of the oil?" The greatest need is to make room when God makes it. Look around you at your situation. Are you not encompassed with needs at this very moment, and almost overwhelmed with difficulties, trials and emergencies? These are all divinely provided vessels for the Holy Spirit to fill, and if you would but rightly understand their meaning, they would become opportunities for receiving new blessings and deliverances which you can get in no other way.

Bring these vessels to God. Hold them steadily before Him in faith and prayer. Keep still, and stop your own restless working until He begins to work. Do nothing that He does not Himself command you to do. Give Him a chance to work, and He will surely do so, and the very trials that threatened to overcome you with discouragement and disaster, will become God's opportunity for the revelation of His grace and glory in your life, as you have never known Him before. "Bring them (all needs) to Me."

JULY 24.

"The righteousness of the law might be fulfilled in us" (Rom. vii. 4).

In our earlier experiences we know the Holy Ghost only at a distance, in things that happen in a providential direction, or in the Word alone, but after awhile we receive Him as an inward Guest, and He dwells in our very midst, and He speaks to us in the innermost chambers of our being. But then the external working of His power does not cease, but it only increases, and seems the more glorious. The Power that dwells within us works without us, answering prayer, healing sickness, overruling providences, "Doing exceeding abundantly above all that we ask or think, according to the Power that worketh in us."

There is a double presence of the Lord for the consecrated believer. He is present in the heart, and is mightily present in the events of life. He is the Christ in us, the Christ of all the days, with all power in heaven and earth.

And so the Holy Ghost is our wonder-worker, our all sufficient God and Guardian, and He is waiting in these days to work as mightily in the affairs of men as in the days of Moses, of Daniel and of Paul.

113

JULY 25.

"He that in these things serveth Christ is acceptable to God" (Rom. xiv. 18).

God can only use us while we are right. Satan cared far less for Peter's denial of his Master than for the use he made of it afterwards to destroy his faith. So Jesus said to him: "I have prayed for thee that thy faith fail not." It was Peter's faith he attacked, and so it is our faith that Satan contests. "The trial of our faith is much more precious than gold that perisheth."

Whatever else we let go let us hold steadfastly to our trust. "Cast not away, therefore, your confidence," and "hold fast the rejoicing of our hope firm unto the end." And if you would hold your trust, hold your sweetness, your rightness of spirit, your obedience to Christ, your victory in every way.

Whatever comes, regard it as of less consequence, than that you should triumph and stand fast, and accepting every circumstance as God is pleased to let occur, wave the banner of your victory in the face of every foe, and go on, shouting in His name, "Thanks be unto God that always causeth us to triumph in Christ Jesus."

JULY 26.

"Now mine eye seeth Thee" (Job xlii. 5).

We must recognize the true character of our self-life and its real virulence and vileness. We must consent to its destruction, and we must take it ourselves, as Abraham did Isaac, and lay it at the feet of God in willing sacrifice.

This is a hard work for the natural heart, but the moment the will is yielded and the choice is made, that death is past, the agony is over, and we are astonished to find that the death is accomplished.

Usually the crisis of life in such cases hangs upon a single point. God does not need to strike us in a hundred places to inflict a death wound. There is one point that touches the heart, and that is the point God usually strikes, the dearest thing in our life, the decisive thing in our plans, the citadel of the will, the center of the heart, and when we yield there, there is little left to yield anywhere else, and when we refuse to yield at this point, a spirit of evasion and compromise enters into all the rest of our life. Lord, we take Thee to enable us to will Thy will to be done in all things in our life without and within.

JULY 27.

114

"The building up of the body of Christ" (R. V., Eph. iv. 13).

God is preparing His heroes, and when the opportunity comes He can fit them into their place in a moment and the world will wonder where they came from. Let the Holy Ghost prepare you, dear friend, by all the discipline of life; and when the last finishing touch has been given to the marble, it will be easy for God to put it on the pedestal, and fit it into its niche.

There is a day coming, when, like Othniel, we, too, shall judge the nations, and rule and reign with Christ on the millennial earth; but ere that glorious day can be, we must let God prepare us as He did Othniel at Kirjethsepher, amid the trials of our present life, and in the little victories, the significance of which, perhaps, we little dream. At least, let us be sure of this, that if the Holy Ghost has got an Othniel ready, the Lord of heaven and earth has a throne prepared for him.

Is it for me to be used by His grace,

Helping His kingdom to bring,

Is it for me to inherit a place,

E'en on the throne of my King?

JULY 28.

"Not my will, but Thine" (Luke xxii. 42).

He who once suffered in Gethsemane will be our strength and our victory, too. We may fear, we may also sink, but let us not be dismayed, and we shall yet praise Him, and look back from a finished course, and say, "Not one word hath failed of all that the Lord hath spoken."

But in order to do this, we must, like Him, meet the conflict, not with a defiant, but with a submissive spirit. He had to say, "Not My will, but Thine be done"; but in saying it, He gained the very thing He surrendered. So the submission of Gethsemane is not a blind and dead submission of a heart that abandons all its hope; but it is the free submission that bows the head, in order to get double strength through the faith and prayer.

We let go, in order that we may take a firmer hold. We give up, in order that we may more fully receive. We lay our Isaac on Mount Moriah, and we ask him back, no longer our Isaac, but God's Isaac, and infinitely more secure, because given back in the resurrection life.

JULY 29.

115

"My helpers in Christ Jesus" (Rom. xvi. 3).

Christ's Church is overrun with captains. She is in great need of a few more privates. A few rivers run into the sea, but a larger number run into other rivers. We cannot all be pioneers, but we can all be helpers, and no man is fitted to go in the front until he has learned well how to go second.

A spirit of self-importance is fatal to all work for Christ. The biggest enemy of true spiritual power is spiritual self-consciousness. Joshua must die before Jericho can fall.

God often has to test His chosen servants by putting them in a subordinate place before He can bring them to the front. Joseph must learn to serve in the kitchen and to suffer in prison before he can rise to the throne, and as soon as Joseph is ready for the throne, the throne is always waiting for Joseph. God has more places than accepted candidates. Let us not be afraid to go into the training class, and even take the lowest place, for we shall soon go up, if we really deserve to. Lord, use me so that Thou shalt be glorified and I shall be hid from myself and others.

JULY 30.

"If thou wilt diligently hearken unto the voice of the Lord thy God and wilt keep all His statutes" (Ex. xv. 26).

Sometimes people fail because they have not confidence in the Physician. The very first requirement of this Doctor is, that you trust Him, and trust Him implicitly, so implicitly that you go forward on His bare word, and act as if you had received His healing the moment you claimed His promise. But no one would expect to be healed by an earthly doctor as soon as they obeyed his directions.

You must do what the Great Physician tells you, if you expect Him to make you whole.

You cannot expect to be healed if you are living in sin, any more than you could expect the best physician to cure you while you lived in a malarial climate and inhaled poison with every breath. So you must get up into the pure air of trust and obedience before Christ can make you whole. And then, if you will trust Him, and attend to His directions, you will find that there is balm in Gilead, and that there is a Great Physician there.

116

JULY 31.

"We were troubled on every side" (II. Cor. vii. 5).

Why should God have to lead us thus, and allow the pressure to be so hard and constant?

Well, in the first place, it shows His all-sufficient strength and grace much better than if we were exempt from pressure and trial. "The treasure is in earthen vessels, that the excellency of the power may be of God, and not of us."

It make us more conscious of our dependence upon Him. God is constantly trying to teach us our dependence, and to hold us absolutely in His hand and hanging upon His care.

This was the place where Jesus Himself stood and where He wants us to stand, not with a self-constituted strength, but with a hand ever leaning upon His, and a trust that dare not take one step alone.

It teaches us trust. There is no way of learning faith except by trial. It is God's school of faith, and it is far better for us to learn to trust God than to enjoy life.

The lesson of faith, once learned, is an everlasting acquisition and an eternal fortune made; and without trust even riches will leave us poor.

AUGUST 1.

"For we must all appear before the judgment seat of Christ; that every one may receive the things done in his body, according to that he hath done" (II Cor. v. 10).

It will not always be the day of toil and trial. Some day, we shall hear our names announced before the universe, and the record read of things that we had long forgotten. How our hearts will thrill, and our heads will bow, as we shall hear our own names called, and then the Master shall recount the triumph and the services which we had ourselves forgotten! And, perhaps, from the ranks of the saved He shall call forward the souls that we have won for Christ and the souls that they in turn had won, and as we see the issue of things that have, perhaps, seemed but trifling at the time, we shall fall before the throne, and say, "Not unto us, O Lord, not unto us, but unto Thy name give glory!"

Beloved, the pages are going up every day, for the record of our life. We are setting the type ourselves, by every moment's action. Hands unseen are stereotyping the plates, and soon the record will be registered, and read before the audience of the universe. and amid the issues of eternity.

AUGUST 2.

"Thy gentleness hath made me great" (Ps. xviii. 35).

The blessed Comforter is gentle, tender, and full of patience and love. How gentle are God's dealings even with sinners! How patient His forbearance! How tender His discipline, with His own erring children! How He led Jacob, Joseph, Israel, David, Elijah, and all His ancient servants, until they could truly say, "Thy gentleness hath made me great."

The heart in which the Holy Spirit dwells will always be characterized by gentleness, lowliness, quietness, meekness, and forbearance. The rude, sarcastic spirit, the brusque manner, the sharp retort, the unkind cut--all these belong to the flesh, but they have nothing in common with the gentle teaching of the Comforter.

The Holy Dove shrinks from the noisy, tumultuous, excited, and vindictive spirit, and finds His home in the lowly breast of the peaceful soul. "The fruit of the Spirit is gentleness, meekness."

Lord, make me gentle. Hush my spirit. Refine my manner. Let me have Christ in my bearing and my very tones as well as in my heart.

AUGUST 3.

"Humble yourselves therefore under the mighty hand of God" (I. Peter v. 6).

The pressure of hard places makes us value life. Every time our life is given back to us from such a trial, it is like a new beginning, and we learn better how much it is worth, and make more of it for God and man.

The pressure helps us to understand the trials of others, and fits us to help and sympathize with them.

There is a shallow, superficial nature, that gets hold of a theory or a promise lightly, and talks very glibly about the distrust of those who shrink from every trial; but the man or woman who has suffered much never does this, but is very tender and gentle, and knows what suffering really means.

This is what Paul meant when he said, "Death worketh in us, but life in you." Trials and hard places are needed to press us forward; even as the furnace fires in the hold of that mighty ship give the force that moves the piston, drives the engine, and propels that great vessel across the sea, in the face of the winds and waves.

AUGUST 4.

"Ye are not in the flesh but in the Spirit if so be that the Spirit of God dwell in you. Now if any man have not the Spirit of Christ he is none of His" (Rom. viii. 9).

A spiritual man is not so much a man possessing a strong spiritual character as a man filled with the Holy Spirit. So the apostle said: "Ye are not in the flesh, but in the Spirit, if so be that the Spirit of God dwelleth in you."

The glory of the new creation, then, is not only that it recreates the human spirit, but that it fits it for the abode of God Himself, and makes it dependent upon the sun, as the child upon the mother. The highest spirituality, therefore, is the most utter helplessness, the most entire dependence and the most complete possession of the Holy Spirit. Therefore, the beautiful act of Christ in breathing upon His disciples, and imparting to them from His own lips the very Spirit that was already in Him, expressed in the most vivid manner the crowning glory of the new creation. And when the Holy Spirit thus possesses us, He fills every part of our being.

AUGUST 5.

"If any man hear My voice and open the door I will come into him and will sup with him and he with Me" (Rev. iii. 20).

Some of us are starving, and wondering why the Holy Spirit does not fill us. We have plenty coming in, but we do not give it out. Give out the blessing you have, start larger plans for service and blessing, and you will soon find that the Holy Ghost is before you, and He will "prevent you with the blessings of goodness," and give you all that He can trust you to give away to others.

There is a beautiful fact in nature which has its spiritual parallels. There is no music so heavenly as an Aeolian harp, and the Aeolian harp is nothing but a set of musical cords arranged in harmony, and then left to be touched by the unseen fingers of the wandering winds. And as the breath of heaven floats over the chords, it is said that notes almost divine float out upon the air, as if a choir of angels were wandering around and touching the strings.

119

And so it is possible to keep our hearts so open to the touch of the Holy Spirit that He can play upon them at will, as we quietly wait in the pathway of His service.

AUGUST 6.

"As many as are led by the Spirit of God they are the sons of God" (Rom. viii. 14).

The blessed Holy Spirit is our Guide, our Leader, and our Resting-place. There are times when He presses us forward into prayer, into service, into suffering, into new experiences, new duties, new claims of faith, and hope, and love, but there are times when He arrests us in our activity, and rests us under His overshadowing wing, and quiets us in the secret place of the Most High, teaching us some new lessons, breathing into us some deeper strength or fulness, and then leading us on again, at His bidding alone. He is the true Guide of the saint, and the true Leader of the Church, our wonderful Counsellor, our unerring Friend; and he who would deny the personal guidance of the Holy Ghost in order that he might honor the Word of God as our only guide, must dishonor that other word of promise, that His sheep shall know His voice, and that His hearkening and obedient children shall hear a voice behind them saying, "This is the way, walk ye in it."

AUGUST 7.

"Knowing this that our old man is crucified" (Rom. vi. 6).

It is purely a matter of faith, and faith and sight always differ, so that to your senses it does not seem to be so, but your faith must still reckon it so. This is a very difficult attitude to hold, and only as we thoroughly believe God can we thus reckon upon His Word and His working, but as we do so, faith will convert it into fact, and it will be even so.

These two words, "yield" and "reckon," are passwords into the resurrection life. They are like the two edges of the "Sword of the Spirit" through which we enter into crucifixion with Christ.

This act of surrender and this reckoning of faith are recognized in the New Testament as marking a very definite crisis in the spiritual life. It does not mean that we are expected to be going through a continual dying, but that there should be one very definite act of dying, and then a constant habit of reckoning ourselves as dead, and meeting everything from this standpoint.

"Reckon yourselves dead indeed unto sin, but alive unto God, through Jesus Christ."

AUGUST 8.

"Be like the dove" (Jer. xlviii. 28).

Harmless as a dove, is Christ's interpretation of the beautiful emblem. And so the Spirit of God is purity itself. He cannot dwell in an unclean heart. He cannot abide in the natural mind. It was said of the anointing of old, "On man's flesh it shall not be poured."

The purity which the Holy Spirit brings is like the white and spotless little plant which grows up out of the heap of manure, or the black soil, without one grain of impurity adhering to its crystalline surface, spotless as an angel's wing.

So the Holy Spirit gives a purity of heart which gives its own protection, for it is essentially unlike the evil things which grow around it. It may be surrounded on every side with evil, but it is uncontaminated and pure because its very nature is essentially holy and divine. Like the plumage of the dove, it cannot be soiled, but comes forth from the miry pool unstained and unsullied by the dark waters, because it is protected by the oily covering which sheds off every defilement and makes it proof against the touch of every stain.

AUGUST 9.

"He shall lay both his hands upon the head of the live goat, and confess over him all the iniquities of the children of Israel; transgressions and sins" (Lev. xvi. 21).

As any evil comes up, and the consciousness of any unholy thing touches our inner senses, it is our privilege at once to hand it over to the Holy Ghost and to lay it upon Jesus, as something already crucified with Him, and as of old, in the case of the sin offering, it will be carried without the camp and burned to ashes.

There may be deep suffering, there may be protracted pain, it may be intensely real; but throughout all there will be a very sweet and sacred sense of God's presence, and intense purity in our whole spirit, and our separation from the evil which is being consumed. Truly, it will be borne without the camp, and even without the smell of the flames upon our garments.

121

It is so blessed to have the Holy Spirit slay things. No swords but His can pass so perfectly between us and the evil, so that it consumes the sin without touching the spirit.

Lord Jesus, my Sin Offering, I lay my sin, my self, my whole nature, upon Thy Cross. Consume me by Thy holy fire, and let me die to all but Thee!

AUGUST 10.

"There is no spot in thee" (Song of Solomon iv. 7).

The blessed Holy Spirit who possesses the consecrated heart is intensely concerned for our highest life, and watches us with a sensitive, and even a jealous love. Very beautiful is the true translation of that ordinary passage in the Epistle of James, "The Spirit that dwelleth in us loveth us to jealousy."

The heart of the Holy Ghost is intensely concerned in preserving us from every stain and blemish, and bringing us into the very highest possibilities of the will of God.

The Heavenly Bridegroom would have His Church not only free from every spot, but also from "every wrinkle, or any such thing." The spot is the mark of sin, but the wrinkle is the sign of weakness, age, and decay, and He wants no such defacing touch upon the holy features of His Beloved; and so the Holy Ghost, who is the Executor of His will, and the Divine Messenger whom He sends to call, separate, and bring home His Bride, is jealously concerned in fulfilling in us all the Master's will.

Lord, take from me every blemish and mark of weakness and decay, and make me Thy spotless Bride.

AUGUST 11.

"All the land which thou seest" (Gen. xiii. 15).

The actual provisions of His grace come from the inner vision.

He who puts the instinct in the bosom of yonder bird to cross the continent in search of summer sunshine in yonder Southern clime is too good to deceive it, and just as surely as He has put the instinct in its breast, so has He also put the balmy breezes and the vernal sunshine yonder to meet it when it arrives.

He who gave to Abraham the vision of the Land of Promise, also said in infinite truth and love: "All the land that thou seest will I give thee." He who breathes into our hearts the heavenly hope, will not deceive or fail us when we press forward to its realization. There is nothing unfaithful in Him who has said: "If it were not so, I would have told you," and we may know that He never will deceive us nor fail us, but all that He reveals by His Holy Spirit He will make our own, as we press forward and enter into its realization.

Lord, give me first the vision and then the victory. Show me all my inheritance, and then give it all to me in Christ Jesus.

AUGUST 12.

"Not ourselves, but Christ Jesus" (II. Cor. iv. 5).

Your Christian influence, your reputation as a worker for God, and your standing among your brethren, may be an idol to which you must die, before you can be free to live for Him alone.

If you have ever noticed the type on a printed page, you must have seen that the little "_i_" has always a dot over it, and it is that dot that elevates it above the other letters in the line.

Now, each us us is a little _i_, and over every one of us there is a little dot of self-importance, self-will, self-interest, self-confidence, self-complacency, or something to which we cling and for which we contend, which just as surely reveals self-life as if it were a mountain of real importance.

This _i_ is a rival of Jesus Christ, and the enemy of the Holy Ghost, and of our peace and life, and therefore God has decreed its death, and the Holy Spirit, with His flaming sword is waiting to destroy it, that we may be able to enter through the gates and come to the Tree of Life. Lord, crowd me out by Thy fulness even as the glory of the Lord left no room for Moses in the Tabernacle.

AUGUST 13.

"Clouds and darkness are round about Him" (Ps. xcvii. 2).

The presence of clouds upon your sky, and trials in your path, is the very best evidence that you are following the pillar of cloud, and walking in the presence of God. They had to enter the cloud before they could behold the glory of the transfiguration, and a little later that same cloud became the chariot to receive the ascending Lord, and it is still waiting as the chariot that will bring His glorious appearing.

Still it is true that white "clouds and darkness are round about His throne, mercy and truth" are ever in their midst, and "shall go before His face."

123

Perhaps the most beautiful and gracious use of the cloud was to shelter them from the fiery sun. Like a great umbrella, that majestic pillar spread its canopy above the camp, and became a shielding shadow from the burning heat in the treeless desert. No one who has never felt an Oriental sun can fully appreciate how much this means--a shadow from the heat.

So the Holy Spirit comes between us and the fiery, scorching rays of sorrow and temptation.

AUGUST 14.

"Touch not Mine anointed, and do My prophets no harm" (Ps. cv. 15).

I would rather play with the forked lightning, or take in my hands living wires, with their fiery current, than speak a reckless word against any servant of Christ, or idly repeat the slanderous darts which thousands of Christians are hurling on others, to the hurt of their own souls and bodies.

You may often wonder, perhaps, why your sickness is not healed, your spirit filled with the joy of the Holy Ghost, or your life blessed and prosperous. It may be that some dart which you have flung with angry voice, or in an idle hour of thoughtless gossip, is pursuing you on its way, as it describes the circle which always bring back to the source from which it came every shaft of bitterness, and every idle and evil word.

Let us remember that when we persecute or hurt the children of God, we are but persecuting Him, and hurting ourselves far more.

Lord, make me as sensitive to the feelings and rights of others as I have often been to my own, and let me live and love like Thee.

AUGUST 15.

"He will guide you into all truth" (John xvi. 13).

The Holy Ghost does not come to give us extraordinary manifestations, but to give its life and light, and the nearer we come to Him, the more simple will His illumination and leading be. He comes to "guide us into all truth." He comes to shed light upon our own hearts, and to show us ourselves. He comes to reveal Christ, to give, and then to illumine, the Holy Scriptures, and to make Divine realities vivid and clear to our spiritual apprehension. He comes as a Spirit of wisdom and revelation in the knowledge of Christ, to "enlighten the eyes of our understanding, that we may know what is the hope of His calling, and what the riches of the glory of His inheritance in the saints, and what is the exceeding greatness of His power to us-ward who believe, according to the working of His mighty power."

Spirit of Power! with heavenly fire,
Our souls endue, our tongues inspire;
Stretch forth Thy mighty Hand,
Thy Pentecostal gifts restore,
The wonders of Thy power once more
Display in every land.

AUGUST 16.

"I am with you alway" (Matt. xxviii. 20).

Oh, how it helps and comforts us in the plod of life to know that we have with us the Christ who spent the first thirty years of His life in the carpenter shop at Nazareth, swinging the hammer, covered with sweat and grimy dust, physically weary as we often are, and able to understand all our experiences of drudgery and labor! and One who still loves to share our common tasks and equip us for our difficult undertakings of hand and brain!

Yes, humble sister, He will help you at the washboard and the kitchen-sink as gladly as at the hour of prayer. Yes, busy mechanic, He will go with you and help you to swing the hammer, or handle the saw, or hold the plow in the toil of life, and you shall be a better mechanic, a more skilled workman, and a more successful man, because you take His wisdom for the common affairs of life. There is no place or time where He is not able and willing to walk by our side, to work through our hands and brains, and to unite Himself in loving and all-sufficient partnership with all our needs and tasks and trials, and prove our all-sufficiency for all things.

AUGUST 17.

"Speak ye unto the Rock" (Num. xx. 8).

The Holy Ghost is very sensitive, as love always is. You can conquer a wild beast by blows and chains, but you cannot conquer a woman's heart that way, or win the love of a sensitive nature; that must be wooed by the delicate touches of trust and affection. So the Holy Ghost has to be taken by a faith as delicate and sensitive as the gentle heart with whom it is coming in touch. One thought of unbelief, one expression of impatient distrust or fear, will instantly check the perfect freedom of His operations as much as a breath of frost would wither the petals of the most sensitive rose or lily.

Speak to the Rock, do not strike it. Believe in the Holy Ghost and treat Him with the tenderest confidence and the most unwavering trust, and He will meet you with instant response and confidence.

Beloved, have you come to the rock in Kadesh? Have you opened all your being to the fulness of the Spirit, and then, with the confidence of the child to the mother, the bride to the husband, the flower to the sunshine, have you received by faith, and are you drinking of His blessed life?

AUGUST 18.

"The three hundred blew the trumpets" (Judges vii. 22).

We little dream, sometimes, what a hasty word, a thoughtless speech, an imprudent act, or a confession of unbelief and fear may do to hinder our highest usefulness, or turn it aside from some great opportunity which God has been preparing for us.

Although the Holy Ghost uses weak men, He does not want them to be weak after He chooses and calls them. Although He uses the foolish things to confound the wise, He does not want us to be foolish after He comes to give us His wisdom and grace. He uses the foolishness of preaching, but, not necessarily, the foolishness of preachers. Like the electric current, which can supply the strength of a thousand men, it is necessary that it should have a proper conductor, and a very small wire is better than a very big rope.

God wants fit instruments for His power--wills surrendered, hearts trusting, lives consistent, and lips obedient to His will; and then He can use the weakest weapons, and make them mighty through God to the pulling down of strongholds.

AUGUST 19.

"Have faith in God" (Mark xi. 22).

He requires of us a perfect faith, and He tells us that if we believe and doubt not, we shall have whatsoever we ask. The faintest touch of unbelief will neutralize our trust.

126

But how shall we have such perfect faith? Is it possible for human nature? Nay, but it is possible to the Divine nature, it is possible to the Christ within us. It is possible for God to give it; and God does give it. But Christ is the Author and Finisher of our faith, and He bids us have the faith of God, and as we have it through the imparting of the Spirit of Christ, we believe even as He.

We pray in His name, and in His very nature, and we live by the faith of the Son of God who loved us and gave Himself for us. The love that He requires of us is not mere human love, nor even the standard of love required in the Old Testament, but something far higher. The new commandment is, Love one another, not as yourselves, but as I have loved you.

How shall such love be made possible? Herein is our love made perfect, because as He is so are we also in this world. Our love is simply His love wrought in us, and imparted to us through the Spirit.

AUGUST 20.

"Herein is My Father glorified" (John xv. 8).

The true way to glorify God is, for God to show His glory through us, to shine through us as empty vessels reflecting His fulness of grace and power.

The sun is glorified when he has a chance to show his light through the crystal window, or reflect it from the spotless mirror or the glassy sea.

There is nothing that glorifies God so much as for a weak and helpless man or woman to be able to triumph, through His strength, in places where the highest human qualities will fail us, and carry in Divine power through every form of toil and suffering, a spirit naturally weak, irresolute, selfish, and sinful, transformed into sweetness, purity, power and standing victorious amid circumstances from which its natural qualities must utterly unfit it. A mind not naturally wise or strong, directed by a Divine wisdom, and carried along the line of a great and mighty plan, and used to accomplish stupendous results for God and man--this is what glorifies God.

So let me glorify my Lord this day and adorn the doctrine of God in all things.

AUGUST 21.

"The battle is not yours" (II. Chron. xx. 15).

The thing is to count the battle God's. "The battle is not yours, but God's." Ye shall not need to fight in this battle. As long as we count the dangers and

127

responsibilities ours, we shall be distracted with fear, but when we realize He is bound to take care of us, as His property and His representatives, we shall feel infinite relief and security.

If I send my servant on a long journey I am responsible for his expenses and protection, and if God sends me anywhere, He is responsible. If we belong to God, and put our life, our family, and our all in His hands, we may know He will take care of us.

If our body belongs to Him, it is His interest to keep us well, just as much as it is for the interest of the shepherd to have his sheep well fed and well cared for, and a credit to him.

"Thanks be unto God who always causeth us to triumph."

Stand up, stand up for Jesus,

Stand in His strength alone;

The arm of flesh will fail you,

Ye dare not trust your own.

AUGUST 22.

"I the Lord, the first and with the last" (Isa. xli. 4).

Thousands of people get stranded after they have embarked on the great voyage of holiness, because they have depended upon the experience rather than on the Author of it. They had supposed that they were thoroughly and permanently delivered from all sin, and in the ecstacy of their first experience they imagine that they shall never again be tried and tempted as before, and when they step out into the actual facts of Christian life and find themselves failing and falling, they are astonished and perplexed, and they conclude that they must have been mistaken in their experience, and so they make a new attempt at the same thing, and again fall, until at last, worn out, with the experiment, they conclude that the experience is a delusion, or, at least, that it was never intended for them, and so they fall back into the old way, and their last state is worse than the first.

What men and women need to-day is to know, not sanctification as a state, but Christ as a living Person.

Lord Jesus, give me Thy heart, Thy faith, Thy life, Thyself.

AUGUST 23.

"Even as He is pure" (I. John iii. 3).

128

God is now aiming to reproduce in us the pattern which has already appeared in Jesus Christ, the Son of God. The Christian life is not an imitation of Christ, but a direct new creation in Christ, and the union with Christ is so complete that He imparts His own nature to us and lives His own life in us and then it is not an imitation, but simply the outgrowth of the nature implanted within.

We live Christ-like because we have the Christ-life. God is not satisfied with anything less than perfection. He required that from His Son. He requires it from us, and He does not, in the process of grace, reduce the standard, but He brings us up to it. He does not let down the righteousness of the law, but He requires of us a righteousness that far exceeds the righteousness of the Scribes and Pharisees, and then He imparts it to us. He counts us righteous in sanctification, and He says of the new creation, "He that doeth righteousness is righteous even as He is righteous."

Lord, live out thy very life in me.

AUGUST 24.

"Let your moderation be known unto all men" (Phil. iv. 5).

The very test of consecration is our willingness not only to surrender the things that are wrong, but to surrender our rights, to be willing to be subject. When God begins to subdue a soul, He often requires us to yield the things that are of little importance in themselves, and thus break our neck and subdue our spirit.

No Christian worker can ever be used of God until the proud self-will is broken, and the heart is ready to yield to God's every touch, no matter through whom it may come.

Many people want God to lead them in their way and they will brook no authority or restraint. They will give their money, but they want to dictate how it shall be spent. They will work as long as you let them please themselves, but let any pressure come and you immediately run up against, not the grace of resignation, but a letter of resignation, withdrawing from some important trust, and arousing a whole community of criticising friends, equally disposed to have their own opinions and their own will about it. It is destructive of all real power.

AUGUST 25.

129

"And I will put My Spirit within you, and cause you to walk in My statutes, and ye shall keep My judgments and do them" (Ezek. xxxvi. 27).

This is a great deal more than a new heart. This a heart filled with the Holy Ghost, the Divine Spirit, the power that causes us to walk in God's commandments.

This is the greatest crisis that comes to a Christian's life, when into the spirit that was renewed in conversion, God Himself comes to dwell and make it His abiding place, and hold it by His mighty power in holiness and righteousness.

Now, after this occurs, one would suppose that we would be lifted into a much more hopeful and exuberant spirit, but the prophet gives a very different picture. He says when this comes to pass we shall loathe ourselves in our own eyes.

The revelation of God gives a profound sense of our own nothingness and worthlessness, and lays us on our face in the dust in self-abnegation.

The incoming of the Holy Ghost displaces self and disgraces self forever, and the highest holiness is to walk in self-renunciation.

AUGUST 26.

"Thine handmaid hath not anything in the house save a pot of oil" (II. Kings iv. 2).

He asked her, "What hast thou in the house?" And she said, "Nothing but a pot of oil." But that pot of oil was adequate for all her wants, if she had only known how to use it.

In truth it represented the Holy Spirit, and the great lesson of the parable is that the Holy Ghost is adequate for all our wants, if we only know how to use Him.

All that she needed was to get sufficient vessels to hold the overflow, and then to pour out until all were filled.

And so the Holy Spirit is limited only by our capacity to receive Him, and when God wants us to have a larger fulness, He has to make room for it by creating greater needs.

God sends us new vessels to be filled with His Holy Spirit in the needs that come to us, and the trials that meet us. These are God's opportunities for God to give us more of Himself, and as we meet them He comes to us in larger fulness for each new necessity.

130

Lord, help me to see Thee in all my trying situations and to make them vessels to hold more of Thy grace.

AUGUST 27.

"Take no thought for your life" (Matt. vi. 25).

Still the Lord is using the things that are despised. The very names of Nazarene and Christian were once epithets of contempt. No man can have God's highest thought and be popular with his immediate generation. The most abused men are often most used.

There are far greater calamities than to be unpopular and misunderstood. There are far worse things than to be found in the minority. Many of God's greatest blessings are lying behind the devil's scarecrows of prejudice and misrepresentation. The Holy Ghost is not ashamed to use unpopular people. And if He uses them, what need they care for men?

Oh, let us but have His recognition and man's notice will count for little, and He will give us all we need of human help and praise. Let us only seek His will, His glory, His approval. Let us go for Him on the hardest errands and do the most menial tasks. Honor enough that He uses us and sends us. Let us not fear in this day to follow Him outside the camp, bearing His reproach, and by-and-by He will own our worthless name before the myriads of earth and sky.

AUGUST 28.

"According to the power that worketh in us" (Eph. iii. 20).

When we reach the place of union with God, through the indwelling of the Holy Ghost, we come into the inheritance of external blessing and enter upon the land of our possession. Then our physical health and strength come to us through the power of our interior life; then the prayer is fulfilled, that we shall be in health and prosper, as our soul prospereth. Then, with the kingdom of God and His righteousness within us, all things are added unto us.

God's external working always keeps pace with the power that worketh in us. When God is enthroned in a human soul, then the devil and the world soon find it out. We do not need to advertise our power. Jesus could not be hid, and a soul filled with Divine power and purity should become the center of attraction to hungry hearts and suffering lives.

Let us receive Him and recognize Him in His indwelling glory, and then will we appropriate all that it means for our life in all its fulness. Lord, give me the "hiding of Thy power," and let Christ be glorified in me.

AUGUST 29.

"To obey is better than sacrifice" (I. Sam. xv. 22).

Our healing is thus represented as a special recompense for obedience. If, therefore, we would please the Lord and have the reward of those who please Him, there is no service so acceptable to Him as our praise.

Let us ever meet Him with a glad and thankful heart and He will reflect it back in the health of our countenance and the buoyant life and springing health, which is but the echo of a joyful heart.

Further, thankfulness is the best preparation for faith. Trust grows spontaneously in the praiseful heart. Thankfulness takes the sunny side of the street and looks at the bright side of God, and it is only thus that we can ever trust Him. Unbelief looks at our troubles and, of course, they seem like mountains, and faith is discouraged by the prospect. A thankful disposition will always find some cause for cheer, and gloomy one will find a cloud in the brightest sky and a fly in the sweetest ointment. Let us cultivate a spirit of cheerfulness, and we shall find so much in God and in our lives to encourage us that we shall have no room for doubt or fear.

AUGUST 30.

"Happy are ye if ye do them" (John xiii. 17).

You little know the rest that comes from the yielded will, the surrendered choice, the abandoned world, the meek and lowly heart that lets the world go by, and knows that it shall inherit the earth which it has refused! You little know the relish that it gives to the blessing to hunger and thirst after righteousness, and to be filled with a satisfaction that worldly delight cannot afford, and then to rise to the higher blessedness of the merciful, the forgiving, the hearts that have learned that it is "more blessed to give than to receive," and the lives that find that "letting go is twice possessing," and blessing others is to be doubly blessed!

Nay, there is yet one jewel brighter than all the rest in this crown of beatitudes. It is the tear-drop crystallized into the diamond, the blood-drop transfigured into the ruby of heaven's eternal crown. It is the joy of suffering with Jesus, and then

132

forgetting all the sorrow in the overflowing joy, until with the heavenly Pascal we know not which to say first, and so we say them both together, "Tears upon tears, joy upon joy".

AUGUST 31.

"Lead me in the way everlasting" (Ps. cxxxix. 24).

There is often apparently but little difference in two distinct lives between constant victory and frequent victory. But that one little difference constitutes a world of success or failure. The one is the Divine, the other is the human; the one is the everlasting way, the other the transient and the imperfect. God wants to lead us to the way everlasting, and to establish us and make us immovable as He. We little know the seriousness of the slightest surrender. It is but the first step in a downward progression, and God only knows where it shall end.

Let us be "not of them that draw back unto perdition, but of them that believe unto the saving our the soul."

Your victory to-day is but preparing the way for a greater victory to-morrow, and your surrender to-day is opening the door for a more terrible defeat in the days to come. Let us, therefore, whatever we have claimed from our blessed Master, commit it to His keeping, and take Him to establish us and hold us fast in the rejoicing of the hope firm unto the end.

SEPTEMBER 1.

"Afterward that which is spiritual" (I. Cor. xv. 46).

God has often to bring us not only into the place of suffering, and the bed of sickness and pain, but also into the place where our righteousness breaks down and our character falls to pieces, in order to humble us in the dust and show us the need of entire crucifixion to all our natural life. Then, at the feet of Jesus we are ready to receive Him, to abide in Him and depend upon Him alone, and draw all our life and strength each moment from Him, our Living Head.

It was thus that Peter was saved by his very fall, and had to die to Peter that he might live more perfectly to Christ.

Have we thus died, and have we thus renounced the strength of our own self-confidence?

We begin life with the natural, next we come into the spiritual; but then, when we have truly received the kingdom of God and His righteousness, the natural is

133

added to the spiritual, and we are able to receive the gifts of His providence and the blessings of life without becoming centered in them or allowing them to separate us from Him.

SEPTEMBER 2.

"Who hath despised the day of small things" (Zech. iv. 10).

The oak comes out of the acorn, the eagle out of that little egg in the nest, the harvest comes out of the seed; and so the glory of the coming age is all coming out of the Christ life now, even as the majesty of His kingdom was all wrapped up that night in the babe of Bethlehem.

Oh, let us take Him for all our life. Let us be united to His person and His risen body. Let us know what it is to say, "The Lord is for the body and the body is for the Lord"! We are members of His body and His flesh and His bones.

He that gave that little infant, His own blessed babe and His only begotten Son, on that dark winter night to the arms of a cruel and ungrateful world, will not refuse to give Him in all His fulness to your heart if you will but open your heart and give Him right of way and full ownership and possession. Then shall you know in your measure His quickening life, even in this earthly life, and by-and-by your hope shall reach its full fruition when you shall sit with Him on His throne with every fiber of your immortal being even as He.

SEPTEMBER 3.

"The God of Israel hath separated you" (Num. xvi. 9).

The little plant may grow out of a manure heap, and be surrounded by filth, and covered very often with the floating dust that is borne upon the breeze, but its white roots are separated from the unclean soil, and its leaves and flowers have no affinity with the dust that settles upon them; and after a shower of summer rain they throw off every particle of defilement, and look up, as fresh and spotless as before, for their intrinsic nature cannot have any part with these defiling things.

This is the separation which Christ requires and which He gives. There is no merit in my staying from the theater if I want to go. There is no value in my abstaining from the foolish novel or the intoxicating cup, if I am all the time wishing I could have them. My heart is there, and my soul is defiled by the desire for evil things. It is not the world that stains us, but the love of the world. The true Levite is separated from the desire for earthly things, and even if he could, he would not have the forbidden pleasures which others prize.

SEPTEMBER 4.

"Come ye yourselves apart" (Mark vi. 31).

One of the greatest hindrances to spirituality is the lack of waiting upon God. You cannot go through twenty-four hours with two or three breaths of air, in the morning, as you sip your coffee. But you must live in the atmosphere, and you must breathe it all day long. Christians do not wait upon God enough. It needs hours and hours daily of spiritual communion with the Holy Spirit to keep your vitality healthful and full. Every moment should find you breathing out yourself into Christ, and breathing afresh His life, and love and power.

God is waiting to send us the Holy Spirit. He is longing to bless us. His one business is to quicken and sustain our spiritual life. He has nothing else to do with His infinite and great resources. Let us receive Him. Let us live in Him. Let us give to Him the joy of knowing that His infinite grace has not been bestowed in vain, but that we appreciate and improve the blessings which He oft has so freely bestowed.

Lord, help me this day to dwell in Thee as the flower in the sunshine, as the fish in the sea, living in Thy love as the atmosphere and element of my being.

SEPTEMBER 5.

"He breathed on them" (John xx. 22).

The beautiful figure suggested by this passage is full of simple instruction. It is as easy to receive the Holy Ghost as it is to breathe. It almost seems as if the Lord had given them the very impression of breathing, and had said, "Now, this is the way to receive the Holy Ghost."

It is not necessary for you to go to a smallpox hospital to have your lungs contaminated with impure air. It is enough for you to keep in your lungs the air you inhaled a minute ago and it will kill you. All the pure elements have been absorbed from it, and there is nothing left but carbon and other deadly gases and fluids.

Therefore, if you are to be filled with the Holy Spirit, you must first get emptied not only of your old sinful life, but of your old spiritual life. You must get a new breath every moment, or you will die. God wants you to empty out all your being into Him, and then you will take Him in, without needing to try too hard. A vacuum always gets filled, an empty pair of lungs unavoidably breathes in the pure air. If you are only in the true attitude, there will be no trouble about receiving the Holy Ghost.

SEPTEMBER 6.

"Finally, my brethren, rejoice in the Lord" (Phil. iii. 1).

There is no spiritual value in depression. One bright and thankful look at the cross is worth a thousand morbid, self-condemning reflections. The longer you look at evil the more it mesmerizes and defiles you into its own likeness. Lay it down at the cross, accept the cleansing blood, reckon yourself dead to the thing that was wrong, and then rise up and count yourself as if you were another man and no longer the same person; and then, identifying yourself with the Lord Jesus, accept your standing in Him and look in your Father's face as blameless as Jesus. Then out of your every fault will come some lesson of watchfulness or some secret of victory which will enable you some day to thank Him, even for your painful experience.

But praise is a sacrifice, for "it is acceptable to God." It goes up to heaven sweeter than the songs of angels, "a sweet smelling savor to your Lord and King." It should be unintermittent--"the sacrifice of praise continually." One drop of poison will neutralize a whole cup of wine, and make it a cup of death, and one moment of gloom will defile a whole day of sunshine and gladness. Let us "rejoice evermore."

SEPTEMBER 7.

"I will joy in the God of my salvation" (Hab. iii. 18).

The secret of joy is not to wait until you feel happy, but to rise, by an act of faith, out of the depression which is dragging you down, and begin to praise God as an act of choice. This is the meaning of such passages as these: "Rejoice in the Lord alway, and again I say, rejoice"; "I do rejoice; yes, and I will rejoice." "Count it all joy when ye fall into divers temptations." In all these cases there is an evident struggle with sadness and then the triumphs of faith and praise.

Now, this is what is meant--in part, at least--by the sacrifice of praise. A sacrifice is that which costs us something. And when a man or woman has some cherished grudge or wrong and is harboring it, nursing it, dwelling on it, rolling it as a sweet morsel under the tongue, and quite determined to enjoy a miserable time in selfish morbidness and grumbling, it costs us no little sacrifice to throw off the morbid spell, to refuse the suggestions of injury, neglect and the remembrance of unkindness, to rise out of the mood of self-commiseration in wholesome and holy determination, and say, "I will rejoice in the Lord"; I will "count it all joy."

SEPTEMBER 8.

"He that eateth Me, even He shall live by Me" (John vi. 57).

What the children of God need is not merely a lot of teaching, but the Living Bread. The best wheat is not good food. It needs to be ground and baked before it can be digested and assimilated so as to nourish the system. The purest and the highest truth cannot sanctify or satisfy a living soul.

He breathes the New Testament message from His mouth with a kiss of love and a breath of quickening power. It is as we abide in Him, lying upon His bosom and drinking in His very life that we are nourished, quickened, comforted and healed.

This is the secret of Divine healing. It is not believing a doctrine, it is not performing a ceremony, it is not wringing a petition from the heavens by the logic of faith and the force of your will; but it is the inbreathing of the life of God; it is the living touch which none can understand except those whose senses are exercised to know the realities of the world unseen. Often, therefore, a very little truth will bring us much more help and blessing than a great amount of instruction.

SEPTEMBER 9.

"All things are lawful for Me" (I. Cor. x. 23).

I may be perfectly free myself to do many things, the doing of which might hurt my brother and wound his conscience, and love will gladly surrender the little indulgence, that she may save her brother from temptation. There are many questions which are easily settled by this principle.

So there are many forms of recreation which, in themselves might be harmless, and, under certain circumstances, unobjectionable, but they have become associated with worldliness and godlessness, and have proved snares and temptations to many a young heart and life; and, therefore, the law of love would

137

lead you to avoid them, discountenance them, and in no way give encouragement to others to participate in them.

It is just in these things that are not required of us by absolute rules, but are the impulses of a thoughtful love, that the highest qualities of Christian character show themselves, and the most delicate shades of Christian love are manifested.

SEPTEMBER 10.

"Wherefore, receive ye one another as Christ also received us, to the glory of God" (Rom. xv. 7).

This is a sublime principle, and it will give sublimity to life. It is stated elsewhere in similar language, "Whatsoever ye do in word or deed, do all in the name of the Lord Jesus."

This is our high calling, to represent Christ, and act in His behalf, and in His character and spirit, under all circumstances and toward all men. "What would Jesus do?" is a simple question which will settle every difficulty, and always settle it on the side of love.

But we cannot answer this question rightly without having Jesus Himself in our hearts. We cannot _act_ Christ. This is too grave a matter for acting. We must _have_ Christ, and simply be natural and true to the life within us, and that life will act itself out.

Oh, how easy it is to love every one, and see nothing but loveliness when our heart is filled with Christ, and how every difficulty melts away and every one we meet seems clothed with the Spirit within us when we are filled with the Holy Ghost!

SEPTEMBER 11.

"Lo, I am with you all the days, even unto the end of the age" (Matt. xxviii. 20).

It is "all the days," not "always." He comes to you each day with a new blessing. Every morning, day by day, He walks with us, with a love that never tires and a blessing that never grows old. And He is with us "all the days"; it is a ceaseless abiding. There is no day so dark, so commonplace, so uninteresting, but you find Him there. Often, no doubt, He is unrecognized, as He was on the way to Emmaus, until you realize how your heart has been warmed, your love stirred, your Bible so strangely vivified, and every promise seems to speak to you with

138

heavenly reality and power. It is the Lord! God grant that His living presence may be made more real to us all henceforth, and whether we have the consciousness and evidence, as they had a few glorious times in those forty days, or whether we go forth into the coming days, as they did most of their days, to walk by simple faith and in simple duty, let us know at least that the fact is true forevermore, THAT HE IS WITH US, a Presence all unseen, but real, and ready if we needed Him any moment to manifest Himself for our relief.

SEPTEMBER 12.

"The furnace for gold; but the Lord trieth the hearts" (Prov. xvii. 3.)

Remember that temptation is not sin unless it be accompanied with the consent of your will. There may seem to be even the inclination, and yet the real choice of your spirit is fixed immovably against it, and God regards it simply as a solicitation and credits you with an obedience all the more pleasing to Him, because the temptation was so strong.

We little know how evil can find access to a pure nature and seem to incorporate itself with our thoughts and feelings, while at the same time we resist and overcome it, and remain as pure as the sea-fowl that emerges from the water without a single drop remaining upon its burnished wing, or as the harp string, which may be struck by a rude or clumsy hand and gives forth a discordant sound, not from any defect of the harp, but because of the hand that touches it. But let the Master hand play upon it, and it is a chord of melody and a note of exquisite delight.

"In nothing terrified by your adversaries which is to you an evident token of salvation and that of God."

SEPTEMBER 13.

"Think it not strange concerning the fiery trial which is to try you" (I. Peter xii. 16).

Most persons after a step of faith are looking for sunny skies and unruffled seas, and when they meet a storm and tempest they are filled with astonishment and perplexity. But this is just what we must expect to meet if we have received anything of the Lord. The best token of His presence is the adversary's defiance, and the more real our blessing, the more certainly it will be challenged. It is a good thing to go out looking for the worst, and if it comes we are not surprised;

139

while if our path be smooth and our way be unopposed, it is all the more delightful, because it comes as a glad surprise.

But let us quite understand what we mean by temptation. You, especially, who have stepped out with the assurance that you have died to self and sin, may be greatly amazed to find yourself assailed with a tempest of thoughts and feelings that seem to come wholly from within and you will be impelled to say, "Why, I thought I was dead, but I seem to be alive." This, beloved, is the time to remember that temptation, the instigation, is not sin, but only of the evil one.

SEPTEMBER 14.

"For the Lord God will help me, therefore shall I not be confounded; therefore, have I set my face like a flint, and I know I shall not be ashamed" (Isa. l. 7).

This is the language of trust and victory, and it was through this faith, as we are told in a passage in Hebrews, that in His last agony, "Jesus, for the joy that was set before Him, endured the cross, despising the shame." His life was a life of faith, His death was a victory of faith, His resurrection was a triumph of faith, His mediatorial reign is all one long victory of faith, "From henceforth expecting till all His enemies be made His footstool."

And so, for us He has become the pattern of faith, and in every situation of difficulty, temptation and distress has gone before us waving the banner of trust and triumph, and bidding us to follow in His victorious footsteps.

He is the great Pattern Believer. While we must claim our salvation by faith, the Great Forerunner also claimed the world's salvation by the same faith.

Let us therefore consider this glorious Leader our perfect example, and as we follow close behind Him, let us remember where He has triumphed we may triumph, too.

SEPTEMBER 15.

"Though it tarry, wait for it, for it will surely come, and will not tarry" (Hab. ii. 3).

Some things have their cycle in an hour and some in a century; but His plans shall complete their cycle whether long or short. The tender annual which blossoms for a season and dies, and the Columbian aloe, which develops in a century, each is true to its normal principle. Many of us desire to pluck our fruit in June rather than wait until October, and so, of course, it is sour and immature;

140

but God's purposes ripen slowly and fully, and faith waits while it tarries, knowing it will surely come and will not tarry too long.

It is perfect rest to fully learn and wholly trust this glorious promise. We may know without a question that His purposes shall be accomplished when we have fully committed our ways to Him, and are walking in watchful obedience to His every prompting. This faith will give a calm and tranquil poise to the spirit and save us from the restless fret and trying to do too much ourselves.

Wait, and every wrong will righten,

Wait, and every cloud will brighten,

If you only wait.

SEPTEMBER 16.

"I will never leave Thee nor forsake Thee" (Heb. xiii. 5).

It is most cheering thus to know that although we err and bring upon ourselves many troubles that might have been easily averted, yet God does not forsake even His mistaken child, but on his humble repentance and supplication is ever really both to pardon and deliver. Let us not give up our faith because we have perhaps stepped out of the path in which He would have led us. The Israelites did not follow when He called them into the Land of Promise, yet God did not desert them; but during the forty years of their wandering He walked by their side bearing their backsliding with patient compassion, and waiting to be gracious unto them when another generation should have come. "In all their afflictions He was afflicted, but the Angel of His presence saved them; He bare them and carried them all the days of old." And so yet, while our wanderings bring us many sorrows and lose us many blessings, to the heart which truly chooses His, He has graciously said: "I will never leave thee nor forsake thee."

SEPTEMBER 17.

"Thy people shall be a freewill offering in the day of Thy power" (Ps. cx. 3).

This is what the term consecration properly means. It is the voluntary surrender or self-offering of the heart, by the constraint of love to be the Lord's. Its glad expression is, "I am my Beloved's." It must spring, of course, from faith. There must be the full confidence that we are safe in this abandonment, that we are not falling over a precipice, or surrendering ourselves to the hands of a judge, but that we are sinking into a Father's arms and stepping into an infinite

141

inheritance. Oh, it is an infinite inheritance. Oh, it is an infinite privilege to be permitted thus to give ourselves up to One who pledges Himself to make us all that we would love to be, nay, all that His infinite wisdom, power and love will delight to accomplish in us. It is the clay yielding itself to the potter's hands that it may be shaped into a vessel of honor, and meet for the Master's use. It is the poor street waif consenting to become the child of a prince that he may be educated and provided for, that he may be prepared to inherit all the wealth of his guardian.

SEPTEMBER 18.

"We walk by faith, not by sight" (II. Cor. v. 7).

There are heavenly notes which have power to break down walls of adamant and dissolve mountains of difficulty. The song of Paul and Silas burst the fetters of the Philippian gaol; the choir of Jehoshaphat put to flight the armies of the Ammonites, and the song of faith will disperse our adversaries and lift our sinking hearts into strength and victory. Beloved, is it the dark hour with us? the winter of barrenness and gloom? Oh, let us remember that it is God's chosen time for the education of faith and that He conceals beneath the surface, precious and untold harvests of unthought-of fruit! It will not be always winter, it will not be always night, and when the morning comes and spring spreads its verdant mantle over the barren fields then we shall be glad that we did not disappoint our Father in the hour of testing, but that faith had already claimed and seen in the distance the glad fruition which sight now beholds, with a rapture even less than the vision of naked faith.

Lord, help me to believe when I cannot see, and learn from my trials to trust Thee more.

SEPTEMBER 19.

"In due season we shall reap if we faint not" (Gal. vi. 9).

If the least of us could only anticipate the eternal issues that will probably spring from the humblest services of faith, we should only count our sacrifices and labors unspeakable heritages of honor and opportunity, and would cease to speak of trials and sacrifices for God.

The smallest grain of faith is a deathless and incorruptible germ, which will yet plant the heavens and cover the earth with harvests of imperishable glory. Lift

142

up your head, beloved, the horizon is wider than the little circle that you can see. We are living, we are suffering, we are laboring, we are trusting, for the ages yet to come. "Let us not be weary in well doing for in due season we shall reap if we faint not," and with tears of transport we shall cry some day, "Oh, how great is thy goodness which Thou hast laid up for them that fear Thee, which Thou hast wrought for them that trust in Thee before the sons of men."

Help me to-day to live under the powers of the world to come, and to live as a man in heaven walking upon the earth.

SEPTEMBER 20.

"They shall not be ashamed that wait" (Isa. xlix. 23).

Often He calls us aside from our work for a season and bids us be still and learn ere we go forth again to minister. Especially is this so when there has been some serious break, some sudden failure and some radical defect in our work. There is no time lost in such waiting hours. Fleeing from his enemies the ancient knight found that his horse needed to be reshod. Prudence seemed to urge him without delay, but higher wisdom taught him to halt a few minutes at the blacksmith's forge by the way to have the shoe replaced, and although he heard the feet of his pursuers galloping hard behind, yet he waited those minutes until his charger was refitted for his flight, and then, leaping into his saddle just as they appeared a hundred yards away, he dashed away from them with the fleetness of the wind, and knew that his halting had hastened his escape. So often God bids us tarry ere we go, and fully recover ourselves for the next great stage of the journey and work.

Lord, teach me to be still and know that Thou art God and all this day to walk with God.

SEPTEMBER 21.

"Faint, yet pursuing" (Judges viii. 4).

It is a great thing thus to learn to depend upon God to work through our feeble resources, and yet, while so depending, to be absolutely faithful and diligent, and not allow our trust to deteriorate into supineness and indolence. We find no sloth or negligence in Gideon, or his three hundred; though they were weak and few, they were wholly true, and everything in them ready for God to use to the very last. "Faint yet pursuing" was their watchword as they followed and finished their glorious victory, and they rested not until the last of their enemies were destroyed, and even their false friends were punished for their treachery and unfaithfulness.

So God still calls the weakest instruments, but when He chooses and enables them they are no longer weak, but "mighty through God," and faithful through His grace to every trust and opportunity; "trusting," as Dr. Chalmers used to say, "as though all depended upon God, and working as though all depended upon themselves."

Teach me, my blessed Master, to trust and obey.

SEPTEMBER 22.

"We see not yet all things put under Him, but we see Jesus" (Heb. ii. 8, 9).

How true this is to us all! How many things there are that seem to be stronger than we are, but blessed be His name! they are all in subjection under Him, and we see Jesus crowned above them all; and Jesus is our Head, our representative, our other self, and where He is we shall surely be. Therefore when we fail to see anything that God has promised, and that we have claimed in our experience, let us look up and see it realized in Him, and claim it in Him for ourselves. Our side is only half the circle, the heaven side is already complete, and the rainbow of which we see not the upper half, shall one day be all around the throne and take in the other hemisphere of all our now unfinished life. By faith, then, let us enter into all our inheritance. Let us lift up our eyes to the north and to the south, to the east and to the west, and hear Him say, "All the land that thou seest will I give thee." Let us remember that the circle, is complete, that the inheritance is unlimited, and that all things are put under His feet.

SEPTEMBER 23.

"I am the Lord that healeth thee" (Ex. xv. 26).

It is very reasonable that God should expect us to trust Him for our bodies as well as our souls, for if our faith is not practical enough to bring us temporal relief, how can we be educated for real dependence upon God for anything that involves serious risk? It is all very well to talk about trusting God for the distant and future prospect of salvation after death! There is scarcely a sinner in a Christian land that does not trust to be saved some day, but there is no grasp in faith like this. It is only when we come face to face with positive issues and

144

overwhelming forces that we can prove the reality of Divine power in a supernatural life. Hence as an education to our very spirits as well as a gracious provision for our temporal life, God has trained His people from the beginning to recognize Him as the supply of all their needs, and to look to Him as the Physician of their bodies and Father of their spirits. Beloved, have you learned the meaning of Jehovah-rophi, and has it changed your Marah of trial into an Elim of blessing and praise?

SEPTEMBER 24.

"He calleth things that are not as though they were" (Rom. iv. 17).

The Word of God creates what it commands. When Christ says to any of us "Now are ye clean through the word which I have spoken unto you," We are clean. When He says "no condemnation" there is none, though there has been a lifetime of sin before. And when He says, "mighty through God to the pulling down of strongholds," then the weak are strong. This is the part of faith, to take God at His Word, and then expect Him to make it real. A French commander thanked a common soldier who had saved his life and called him captain, although he was but a private, but the man took the commander at his word, accepted the new name and was thereby constituted indeed a captain.

Shall we thus take God's creating word of justification, sanctification, power and deliverance and thus make real the mighty promise, "He giveth power to the faint, and to them that have no might He increaseth strength; for they that wait on the Lord shall renew their strength."

SEPTEMBER 25.

"The faith of the Son of God" (Gal. ii. 20).

Let us learn the secret even of our faith. It is the faith of Christ, springing in our heart and trusting in our trials. So shall we always sing, "The life that I now live I live by the faith of the Son of God, who loved me and gave Himself for me." Thus looking off unto Jesus, "the Author and Finisher of our faith," we shall find that instead of struggling to reach the promises of God, we shall lie down upon them in blessed repose and be borne up by them with the faith which is no more our own than the promises upon which it rests. Each new need will find us leaning afresh on Him for the grace to trust and to overcome.

Further we see here the true spirit of prayer. It is the Spirit of Christ in us. "In the midst of the church will I sing praises unto thee." Christ still sings these praises in the trusting heart and lifts our prayers into songs of victory! This is the true spirit of prayer, like Paul and Silas in the prison at Philippi, turning prayer into praise, night into day, the night of sorrow into the morning of joy, and when He is in us, the spirit of faith, He will also become the spirit of praise.

SEPTEMBER 26.

"I will be with Him in trouble" (Ps. xci. 15).

The question often comes, "Why didn't He help me sooner!" It is not His order. He must first adjust you to the situation and cause you to learn your lesson from it. His promise is, "I will be with him in trouble; I will deliver him and honor him." He must be with you in the trouble first until you grow quiet. Then He will take you out of it. This will not come till you have stopped being restless and fretful about it and become calm and trustful. Then He will say, "It is enough."

God uses trouble to teach His children precious lessons. They are intended to educate us. When their good work is done a glorious recompense will come to us through them. There is a sweet joy and opportunity in them. He does not regard them as difficulties but as opportunities. They have come to give God a greater interest in you, and to show how He can deliver you from them. We cannot have a mercy worth praising God for without difficulty. God is as deep, and long, and high, as our little world of circumstances.

SEPTEMBER 27.

"The glorious liberty of the children of God" (Rom. viii. 21).

Are you above self and self-pleasing in every way? Have you got above circumstances so that you are not influenced by them? Are you above sickness and the evil forces around that would drag down your physical life into the quicksands? These forces are all around, and if yielded to would quickly swamp us. God does not destroy sickness, or its power to hurt, but He lifts us above it. Are you above your feelings, moods, emotions and states? Can you sail immovable as the stars through all sorts of weather? A harp will give out sweet music or discordant sounds as different fingers touch the strings. If the devil's hand is on your harp strings what hideous sounds it will give. Let the fingers of the Lord sweep it, and it will breathe out celestial music. Are you lifted above people, so that you are not bound by or to any one except in the dear Lord, and are you standing free in His glorious life?

"I am risen with Christ, I am dwelling above;
I am walking with Jesus below,
I am shedding the light of His glory and love
Around me wherever I go."

SEPTEMBER 28.

"The trial of your faith being much more precious than gold" (I. Peter i. 7).

Our trials are great opportunities. Too often we look on them as great obstacles. It would be a heaven of rest and an inspiration of unspeakable power if each of us would henceforth recognize every difficult situation as one of God's chosen ways of proving to us His love and power, and if instead of calculating upon defeat we should begin to look around for the messages of His glorious manifestations. Then indeed would every cloud become a rainbow, and every mountain a path of ascension and a scene of transfiguration. If we will look upon the past, many of us will find that the very time our heavenly Father has chosen to do the kindest things for us and give us the richest blessings has been the time when we were strained and shut in on every side. God's jewels are often sent us in rough packages and by dark liveried servants, but within we find the very treasures of the King's palace and the Bridegroom's Love.

Fire of God, thy work begin,
Burn up the dross of self and sin;
Burn off my fetters, set me free,
And through the furnace walk with me.

SEPTEMBER 29.

"Call not thou common" (Acts x. 15).

"There is nothing common of itself" (Rom. xiv. 14).

We can bring Christ into common things as fully as into what we call religious services. Indeed, it is the highest and hardest application of Divine grace, to bring it down to the ordinary matters of life, and therefore God is far more honored in this than even in things that are more specially sacred.

147

Therefore, in the twelfth chapter of Romans, which is the manual of practical consecration, just after the passage that speaks of ministering in sacred things, the apostle comes at once to the common, social and secular affairs into which we are to bring our consecration principles. We read: "Be kindly affectioned one to another with brotherly love; in honor preferring one another; not slothful in business; fervent in spirit; serving the Lord."

God wants the Levites scattered all over the cities of Israel. He wants your workshop, factory, kitchen, nursery, editor's room and printing-office, as much as your pulpit and closet. He wants you to be just as holy at high noon on Monday or Wednesday, as in the sanctuary on Sabbath morning.

SEPTEMBER 30.

"In the secret places of the stairs" (Song of Solomon ii. 14).

The dove is in the cleft of the rock--the riven side of our Lord. There is comfort and security there. It is also in the secret places of the stairs. It loves to build its nest in the high towers to which men mount the winding stairs for hundreds of feet above the ground. What a glorious vision is there obtained of the surrounding scenery. It is a picture of ascending life. To reach its highest altitudes we must find the secret places of the stairs. That is the only way to rise above the natural plane. Our life should be one of quiet mounting with occasional resting places; but we should be mounting higher step by step. Everybody does not find this way of secret ascent. It is for God's chosen ones. The world may think you are going down. You may not have as much public work to do as formerly. "Blessed are the poor in spirit." It is a secret, hidden life. We may be hardly aware that we are growing, till some day a test comes and we find we are established. Have you got above the power of sin so that Christ is keeping you from wilful disobedience? Does it give you a shudder to know the consciousness of sin? Are you lifted above the world?

OCTOBER 1.

"That in the ages to come He might show the exceeding riches of His grace" (Eph. ii. 7).

Christ's great purpose for His people is to train them up to know the hope of their calling, and the riches of the glory of their inheritance and what the exceeding greatness of His power toward us who believe.

Let us prove, in all our varied walks of life, and scenes of conflict, the fulness of His power and grace and thus shall we know "In the ages to come the exceeding riches of His grace in His kindness to us in Jesus Christ."

Beloved, are you thus following your Teacher in the school of faith, and finishing the education which is by and by to fit you for "a far more exceeding and eternal weight of glory"? This is only the School of Faith.

Little can we now dream what these lessons will mean for us some day, when sitting with Him on His throne and sharing with Him the power of God and the government of the universe. Let us be faithful scholars now and soon with Him, we too, will have "endured the cross despising the shame," and shall "sit down at the right hand of the throne of God."

OCTOBER 2.

"Moses gave not any inheritance; the Lord God of Israel was their inheritance, as He said unto them" (Josh. xiii. 33).

This is very significant. God gave the land to the other tribes but He gave Himself to the Levites. There is such a thing in Christian life as an inheritance from the Lord, and there is such a thing as having the Lord Himself for our inheritance.

Some people get a sanctification from the Lord which is of much value, but which is variable, and often impermanent. Others have learned the higher lesson of taking the Lord Himself to be their keeper and their sanctity, and abiding in Him they are kept above the vicissitudes of their own states and feelings.

Some get from the Lord large measures of joy and blessing, and times of refreshing.

Others, again, learn to take the Lord Himself as their joy.

Some people are content to have peace with God, but others have taken "the peace of God that passeth all understanding."

Some have faith _in_ God, while others have the faith _of_ God. Some have many touches of healing from God, others, again, have learned to live in the very health of God Himself.

OCTOBER 3.

"The little foxes that spoil the vines" (Song of Solomon, ii. 15).

There are some things good, without being perfect. You don't need to have a whole regiment cannonading outside your room to keep you awake. It is quite enough that your little alarm clock rings its little bell. It is not necessary to fret about everything; it is quite enough if the devil gets your mind rasped with one little worry, one little thought which destroys your perfect peace. It is like the polish on a mirror, or an exquisite toilet table, one scratch will destroy it; and the finer it is the smaller the scratch that will deface it. And so your rest can be destroyed by a very little thing. Perhaps you have trusted in God about your future salvation; but have you about your present business or earthly cares, your money and your family?

What is meant by the peace that passeth all understanding? It does not mean a peace no one can comprehend. It means a peace that no amount of reasoning will bring. You cannot get it by thinking. There may be perfect bewilderment and perplexity all round the horizon, but yet your heart can rest in perfect security because He knows, He loves, He leads.

OCTOBER 4.

"Instead of the brier, the myrtle tree" (Isa. lv. 13).

God's sweetest memorial is the transformed thorn and the thistle blooming with flowers of peace and sweetness, where once grew recriminations.

Beloved, God is waiting to make just such memorials in your life, out of the things that are hurting you most to-day. Take the grievances, the separations, the strained friendships and the broken ties which have been the sorrow and heartbreak of your life, and let God heal them, and give you grace to make you right with all with whom you may be wrong, and you will wonder at the joy and blessing that will come out of the things that have caused you nothing but regret and pain.

"Blessed are the peacemakers, for they shall be called the children of God." The everlasting employment of our blessed Redeemer is to reconcile the guilty and the estranged from God, and the highest and most Christ-like work that we can do is, to be like Him.

Shall we go forth to dry the tears of a sorrowing world, to heal the broken-hearted, to bind up the wounds of human lives, and to unite heart to heart, and earth to heaven?

150

OCTOBER 5.

"He hath triumphed gloriously" (Ex. xv. 1).

Beloved, God calls us to victory. Have any of you given up the conflict, have you surrendered? Have you said, "This thing is too much"? Have you said, "I can give up anything else but this"? If you have, you are not in the land of promise. God means you should accept every difficult thing that comes in your life. He has started with you, knowing every difficulty. And if you dare to let Him, He will carry you through not only to be conquerors, but "more than conquerors." Are you looking for all the victory?

God gives His children strength for the battle and watches over them with a fond enthusiasm. He longs to fold you to His arms and say to you, "I have seen thy conflict, I have watched thy trials, I have rejoiced in thy victory; thou hast honored Me." You know He told Joshua at the beginning, "There shall not any man be able to stand before thee all the days of thy life; as I was with Moses, so shall I be with thee: I will not fail thee, nor forsake thee." And again, He says to us, "Fear thou not, for I am with thee."

OCTOBER 6.

"Ephraim, he hath mixed himself" (Hos. vii. 8).

It is a great thing to learn to take God first, and then He can afford to give us everything else, without the fear of its hurting us.

As long as you want anything very much, especially more than you want God, it is an idol. But when you become satisfied with God, everything else so loses its charm that He can give it to you without harm, and then you can take just as much as you choose, and use it for His glory.

There is no harm whatever in having money, houses, lands, friends and dearest children, if you do not value these things for themselves.

If you have been separated from them in spirit, and become satisfied with God Himself, then they will become to you channels to be filled with God to bring Him nearer to you. Then every little lamb around your household will be a tender cord to bind you to the Shepherd's heart. Then every affection will be a little golden cup filled with the wine of His love. Then every bank, stock and investment will be but a channel through which you can pour out His benevolence and extend His gifts.

151

OCTOBER 7.

"He opened not His mouth" (Isa. liii. 7).

How much grace it requires to bear a misunderstanding rightly, and to receive an unkind judgment in holy sweetness! Nothing tests a Christian character more than to have some evil thing said about him. This is the file that soon proves whether we are electro-plate or solid gold. If we could only know the blessings that lie hidden in our lives, we would say, like David, when Shimei cursed him, "Let him curse; it may be the Lord will requite me good for his cursing this day."

Some people get easily turned aside from the grandeur of their life-work by pursuing their own grievances and enemies, until their life gets turned into one little petty whirl of warfare. It is like a nest of hornets. You may disperse the hornets, but you will probably get terribly stung, and get nothing for your pains, for even their honey is not worth a search.

God give us more of His Spirit, who, when reviled, reviled not again; but committed Himself to Him that judgeth righteously.

Consider Him that endured such contradiction of sinners against Himself.

OCTOBER 8.

"There failed not aught of any good thing which the Lord had spoken" (Josh. xxi. 45).

Some day, even you, trembling, faltering one, shall stand upon those heights and look back upon all you have passed through, all you have narrowly escaped, all the perils through which He guided you, the stumblings through which He guarded you, and the sins from which He saved you; and you shall shout, with a meaning you cannot understand now, "Salvation unto Him who sitteth upon the throne, and unto the Lamb."

Some day He will sit down with us in that glorious home, and we shall have all the ages in which to understand the story of our lives. And He will read over again this old marked Bible with us, He will show us how He kept all these promises, He will explain to us the mysteries that we could not understand, He will recall to our memory the things we have long forgotten, He will go over again with us the book of life, He will recall all the finished story, and I am sure we will often cry: "Blessed Christ! you have been so true, you have been so good! Was there ever love like this?" And then the great chorus will be repeated once more--"There failed not aught of any good thing that He hath spoken; all came to pass."

OCTOBER 9.

"Peace be unto you" (John xx. 19, 21).

This is the type of His first appearing to our hearts when He comes to bring us His peace and to teach us to trust Him and love Him.

But there is a second peace which He has to give. Jesus said unto them again, "Peace be unto you." There is a "peace," and there is an "again peace." There is a peace with God, and there is "the peace of God that passeth understanding." It is the deeper peace that we need before we can serve Him or be used for His glory.

While we are burdened with our own cares, He cannot give us His. While we are occupied with ourselves, we cannot be at leisure to serve Him. Our minds will be so filled with our own anxieties that we would not be equal to the trust which He requires of us, and so, before He can entrust us with His work, He wants to deliver us from every burden and anxiety.

"Peace, perfect peace, in this dark world of sin,
The blood of Jesus whispers peace within.
Peace, perfect peace, by thronging duties pressed,
To do the will of Jesus, this is rest."

OCTOBER 10.

"If ye, through the Spirit, do mortify the deeds of the body, ye shall live" (Rom. viii. 13).

The Holy Spirit is the only one who can kill us and keep us dead. Many Christians try to do this disagreeable work themselves, and they are going through a continual crucifixion, but they can never accomplish the work permanently. This is the work of the Holy Spirit, and when you really yield yourself to the death, it is delightful to find how sweetly He can slay you.

By the touch of the electric spark they tell us life is extinguished almost without a quiver of pain. But, however this may be in natural things, we know the Holy Spirit can touch with celestial fire the surrendered thing, and slay it in a moment, after it is really yielded up to the sentence of death. That is our business, and it is God's business to execute that sentence, and to keep it constantly operative.

153

Don't let us live in the pain of perpetual and ineffectual suicide, but reckoning ourselves dead indeed, let us leave ourselves in the hands of the blessed Holy Spirit, and He will slay whatever rises in opposition to His will, and keep us true to our heavenly reckoning, and filled with His resurrection life.

OCTOBER 11.

"And He that searcheth the hearts knoweth what is the mind of the Spirit, because He maketh intercession for the saints according to the will of God" (Rom. viii. 27).

The Holy Spirit becomes to the consecrated heart the Spirit of intercession. We have two Advocates. We have an Advocate with the Father, who prays for us at God's right hand; but the Holy Spirit is the Advocate within, who prays in us, inspiring our petitions and presenting them, through Christ, to God.

We need this Advocate. We know not what to pray for, and we know not how to pray as we ought, but He breathes in the holy heart the desires that we may not always understand, the groanings which we could not utter.

But God understands, and He, with a loving Father's heart, is always searching our hearts to find the Spirit's prayer, and to answer it. He finds many a prayer there that we have not discovered, and answers many a cry that we never understood. And when we reach our home and read the records of life, we shall better know and appreciate the infinite love of that Divine Friend, who has watched within as the Spirit of prayer, and breathed out our every need to the heart of God.

OCTOBER 12.

"The law of the Spirit of life in Christ Jesus hath made me free" (Rom. viii. 2).

The life of Jesus Christ brought into our heart by the Holy Spirit, operates there as a new law of divine strength and vitality, and counteracts, overcomes and lifts us above the old law of sin and death.

Let us illustrate these two laws by a simple comparison. Look at my hand. By the law of gravitation it naturally falls upon the desk and lies there, attracted downward by that natural law which makes heavy bodies fall to the earth.

But there is a stronger law than the law of gravitation--my own life and will. And so through the operation of this higher law--the law of vitality--I defy the law of gravitation, and lift my hand and hold it above its former resting-place,

154

and move it at my will. The law of vitality has made me free from the law of gravitation.

Precisely so the indwelling life of Christ Jesus, operating with the power of a law, lifts me above, and counteracts the power of sin in my fallen nature.

OCTOBER 13.

"The carnal mind is enmity against God" (Rom. viii. 7).

The flesh is incurably bad. "It is not subject to the law of God, neither, indeed, can be." It never can be any better. It is no use trying to improve the flesh. You may educate it all you please. You may train it by the most approved methods, you may set before it the brightest examples, you may pipe to it or mourn to it, treat it with encouragement or severity; its nature will always be incorrigibly the same.

Like the wild hawk which the little child captures in its infancy and tries to train in the habits of the dove, before you are aware it will fasten its cruel beak upon the gentle fingers that would caress it, and show the old wild spirit of fear and ferocity. It is a hawk by nature, and it can never be made a dove. "For the carnal mind is enmity against God. It is not subject to the law of God, neither, indeed, can be."

The only remedy for human nature is to destroy it, and receive instead the divine nature. God does not improve man. He crucifies the natural life with Christ, and creates the new man in Christ Jesus.

OCTOBER 14.

"Get thee, behind me, Satan" (Matt. xvi. 23).

When your old self comes back, if you listen to it, fear it, believe it, it will have the same influence upon you as if it were not dead; it will control you and destroy you. But if you will ignore it and say: "You are not I, but Satan trying to make me believe that the old self is not dead; I refuse you, I treat you as a demon power outside of me, I detach myself from you"; if you treat it as a wife would her divorced husband, saying: "You are nothing to me, you have no power over me, I have renounced you, in the name of Jesus I bid you hence,"--lo! the evil thing will disappear, the shadow will vanish, the wand of faith will lay the troubled spirit, and send it back to the abyss, and you will find that Christ is there instead, with His risen life, to back up your confidence and seal your victory.

155

Satan can stand anything better than neglect. If you ignore him he gets disgusted and disappears. Jesus used to turn His back upon him and say, "Get thee behind Me, Satan." So let us refuse him, and we shall find that he will be compelled to act according to our faith.

OCTOBER 15.

"Faith is the evidence of things not seen" (Heb. xi. 1).

True faith drops its letter in the post-office box, and lets it go. Distrust holds on to a corner of it, and wonders that the answer never comes.

I have some letters in my desk that have been written for weeks, but there was some slight uncertainty about the address or the contents, so they are yet unmailed. They have not done either me or anybody else any good yet. They will never accomplish anything until I let them go out of my hands and trust them to the postman and the mail.

This is the case with true faith. It hands its case over to God, and then He works.

That is a fine verse in the thirty-seventh Psalm: "Commit thy way unto the Lord, trust also in Him, and He worketh." But He never worketh until we commit.

Faith is a receiving, or still better, a taking of God's proffered gifts. We may believe, and come, and commit, and rest, but we will not fully realize all our blessing until we begin to receive and come into the attitude of abiding and taking.

OCTOBER 16.

"Whereas thou hast been forsaken and hated, I will make thee a joy" (Isa. lx. 15).

God loves to take the most lost of men, and make them the most magnificent memorials of His redeeming love and power. He loves to take the victims of Satan's hate, and the lives that have been the most fearful examples of his power to destroy, and to use them to illustrate and illuminate the possibilities of Divine mercy and the new creations of the Holy Spirit.

He loves to take the things in our own lives that have been the worst, the hardest and the most hostile to God, and to transform them so that we shall be the opposites of our former selves.

156

The sweetest spirits are made out of the most stormy and self-willed, the mightiest faith is created out of a wilderness of doubts and fears, and the Divinest love is transformed out of stony hearts of hate and selfishness.

The grace of God is equal to the most uncongenial temperaments, to the most unfavorable circumstances; and its glory is to transform a curse into blessing, and show to men and angels of ages yet to come, that "where sin abounded, there grace did much more abound."

OCTOBER 17.

"Abraham believed God" (Rom. iv. 3).

Abraham's faith reposed on God Himself. He knew the God he was dealing with. It was a personal confidence in one whom he could utterly trust.

The real secret of Abraham's whole life was that he was the friend of God, and knew God to be his great, good and faithful Friend, and, taking Him at His word, he had stepped out from all that he knew and loved, and gone forth upon an unknown pathway with none but God.

Beloved, are we trusting not only in the word of God, but have we learned to lean our whole weight upon Himself, the God of infinite love and power, our covenant God and everlasting Friend?

We are told that Abraham glorified God by this life of faith. The true way to glorify God is to let the world see what He is, and what He can do. God does not want us so much to do things, as to let people see what He can do. God is not looking for extraordinary characters as His instruments, but He is looking for humble instruments through whom He can be honored throughout the ages.

OCTOBER 18.

"All things are naked and open unto the eyes of Him with whom we have to do" (Heb. iv. 13).

The literal translation of this phrase is, all things are stripped and stunned. This is the force of the Greek words. The figure is that of an athlete in the Coliseum who has fought his best in the arena, and has at length fallen at the feet of his adversary, disarmed and broken down in helplessness. There he lies, unable to strike a blow, or lift his arm. He is stripped and stunned, disarmed and disabled, and there is nothing left for him but to lie at the feet of his adversary and throw up his arms for mercy.

Now this is the position that God wants to bring us to, where we shall cease our struggles and our attempts at self-defence or self-improvement, and throw ourselves helplessly upon the mercy of God. This is the sinner's only hope, and when he thus lies at the feet of mercy, Jesus is ready to lift him up and give him that free salvation which is waiting for all.

This, too, is the greatest need of the Christian seeking a deeper and higher life, to come to a full realization of his nothingness and helplessness, and to lie down, stripped and stunned at the feet of Jesus.

OCTOBER 19.

"Denying ungodliness" (Titus ii. 12).

Let us say, "No," to the flesh, the world and the love of self, and learn that holy self-denial in which consists so much of the life of obedience. Make no provision for the flesh; give no recognition to your lower life. Say "No" to everything earthly and selfish. How very much of the life of faith consists in simply denying ourselves.

We begin with one great "Yes," to God, and then we conclude with an eternal "No," to ourselves, the world, the flesh and the devil.

If you look at the ten commandments of the Decalogue, you will find that nearly every one of them is a "Thou shalt not." If you read the thirteenth chapter of First Corinthians, with its beautiful picture of love, you will find that most of the characteristics of love are in the negative, what love "does not, thinks not, says not, is not." And so you will find that the largest part of the life of consecration is really saying, "No."

I am not my own,

I belong to Him.

I am His alone,

I belong to Him.

OCTOBER 20.

"Let us not be weary in well-doing" (Gal. vi. 9).

If Paul could only know the consolation and hope that he has ministered to the countless generations who have marched along the pathway from the cross to the Kingdom above, he would be willing to go through a thousand lives and a

158

thousand deaths such as he endured for the blessing that has followed since his noble head rolled in the dust by the Ostian gate of Rome.

And if the least of us could only anticipate the eternal issues that will probably spring from the humblest services of faith, we should only count our sacrifices and labors unspeakable heritages of honor and opportunity, and would cease to speak of trials and sacrifices made for God.

The smallest grain of faith is a deathless and incorruptible germ, which will yet plant the heavens and cover the earth with harvests of imperishable glory. Lift up your head, beloved, the horizon is wider than the little circle that you can see. We are living, we are suffering, we are laboring, we are trusting, for the ages yet to come!

OCTOBER 21.

"Who shall separate us from the love of Christ?" (Rom. viii. 35).

And then comes the triumphant answer, after all the possible obstacles and enemies have been mentioned one by one, "Nay, in all these things we are more than conquerors, through Him that loved us." Our trials will be turned to helps; our enemies will be taken prisoners and made to fight our battles. Like the weights on yonder clock, which keep it going, our very difficulties will prove incentives to faith and prayer, and occasions for God becoming more real to us.

We shall get out of our troubles not only deliverance but triumph, and in all these things be even more than conquerors through Him that loved us.

Our security depends not upon our unchanging love, but on the love of God in Christ Jesus toward us. It is not the clinging arms of the babe on the mother's breast that keep it from falling, but the strong arms of the mother about it which will never let it go. He has loved us with an everlasting love, and although all else may change, yet He will never leave us nor forsake us.

OCTOBER 22.

"Touched with the feeling of our infirmities" (Heb. iv. 15).

Some of us know a little what it is to be thrilled with a sense of the sufferings of others, and sometimes, the sins of others, and sins that seem to saturate us as they come in contact with us, and throw over us an awful sense of sin and need.

This is, perhaps, intended to give us some faint conception of the sympathy that Jesus felt when He had taken our sins, our sicknesses and our sorrows. Let us

159

not hesitate to lay them on Him! It is far easier for Him to bear them off us than to bear them with us. He has already borne them for us, both in His life and in His death. Let us roll the burden upon Him, and let it roll away, and then, strong in His strength, and rested in His life and love, let us go forth to minister to others the sympathy and help which He has so richly given us.

The world is full of sorrow, and they that have known its bitterness and healing are God's ministers of consolation to a weeping world.

O, the tears that flow around us,
Let us wipe them while we may;
Bring the broken hearts to Jesus,
He will wipe their tears away.

OCTOBER 23.

"How long halt ye between two opinions?" (I. Kings xviii. 21).

It is strange that people will not get over the idea that a consecrated life is a difficult one. A simple illustration will answer this foolish impression. Suppose a street car driver were to say, "It is much easier to run with one wheel on the track and the other off," his line would soon be dropped by the public, and they would prefer to walk. Of course, it is ever so much easier to run with both wheels on the track, and always on the track, and it is much easier to follow Christ fully than to follow with a half heart and halting step. The prophet was right in his pungent question, "How long halt ye between two opinions?" The undecided man is a halting man. The halting man is a lame man and a miserable man, and the out-and-out Christian is the admiration of men and angels, and a continual joy to himself.

Say, is it all for Jesus,
As you so often sing;
Is He your Royal Master,
Is He your heart's true King?

OCTOBER 24.

"First gave their ownselves to the Lord, and unto us by the will of God" (II. Cor. viii. 5).

160

It is essential, in order to be successful in Christian work, that you shall be loyal not only to God, but to the work with which you are associated. The more deeply one knows the Lord the easier it is to get along with Him.

Superficial Christians are apt to be crotchetty. Mature Christians are so near the Lord that they are not afraid of missing His guidance, and not always trying to assert their loyalty to Him and independence of others.

The Corinthians, who had given themselves first to the Lord, had no difficulty in giving themselves to His Apostle by the will of God. It is delightful to work with true hearts on whom we can utterly depend.

God give us the spirit of a sound mind and the heart to "help along."

You can help by holy prayer,

Helpful love and joyful song;

O, the burdens you may bear;

O, the sorrows you may share;

O, the crowns you may yet may wear,

If you help along.

OCTOBER 25.

"Now it is high time to awake out of sleep. Let us cast off the works of darkness and let us put on the armor of light" (Rom. xiii. 11, 12).

Let us wake out of sleep; let us be alert; let us be alive to the great necessities that really concern us.

Let us put off the garments of the night and the indulgences of the night; the loose robes of pleasure and flowing garments of repose; the festal pleasures of the hours of darkness are not for the children of the day. Let us cast off the works of darkness.

Let us arm ourselves for the day. Before we put on our clothes, let us put on our weapons, for we are stepping out into a land of enemies and a world of dangers; let us put on the helmet of salvation, the breastplate of faith and love, and the shield of faith, and stand armed and vigilant as the dangers of the last days gather around us.

Let us put on the Lord Jesus Christ. This is our robe of day. Not our own works or righteousness, but the person and righteousness of the Lord Jesus Christ, who gave us His very life, and becomes to us our All-Sufficiency.

161

OCTOBER 26.

"Go out into the highways and compel them to come in" (Luke xiv. 23).

In the great parable in the fourteenth chapter of Luke, giving an account of the great supper an ancient lord prepared for his friends and neighbors, and to which, when they asked to be excused, he invited the halt and the lame from the city slums and the lepers from outside the gate, there is a significant picture and object lesson of the program of Christianity in this age.

In the first place, it is obvious to every thoughtful mind that the Master is beginning to excuse the Gospel-hardened people of Christian countries. It is getting constantly more difficult to interest the unsaved of our own land, especially those that have been accustomed to hear the Gospel and the things of Christ. They have asked to be excused from the Gospel feast, and the Lord is excusing them.

At the same time, two remarkable movements indicated in the parable are becoming more and more manifest in our time. One is the Gospel for the slums and the neglected classes at home; the other is the Gospel for the heathen or the neglected classes abroad.

OCTOBER 27.

"Behold, I am the Lord, the God of all flesh; is there anything too hard for Me?" (Jer. xxxii. 27.)

Cyrus, the King, was compelled to fulfil the vision of Jeremiah, by making a decree, the instant the prophecy had foretold, declaring that Jehovah had bidden him rebuild Jerusalem and invite her captives to return to their native home. So Jeremiah's faith was vindicated and Jehovah's prophecy gloriously fulfilled, as faith ever will be honored. Oh, for the faith, that in the dark present and the darker future, shall dare to subscribe the evidences and seal up the documents if need be, for the time of waiting, and then begin to testify to the certainty of its hope like the prophet of Anathoth!

The word Anathoth has a beautiful meaning, "echoes." So faith is the "echo" of God and God always gives the "echo" to faith, as He answers it back in glorious fulfilment. Oh, let our faith echo also the brave claim of the ancient prophet and take our full inheritance, with his glorious shout, "Oh, Lord, Thou art the God of all flesh, is there anything too hard for the Lord?" and back like an

162

echo will come the heavenly answer to our heart, "I am the God of all flesh, is there anything too hard for Me?"

OCTOBER 28.

"Thou good servant, because thou hast been faithful in a very little, have thou authority over ten cities" (Luke xix. 17).

It is not our success in service that counts, but our fidelity. Caleb and Joshua were faithful and God remembered it when the day of visitation came. It was a very difficult and unpopular position, and all of us are called in the crisis of our lives to stand alone and in this very matter of trusting God for victory over sin and our full inheritance in Christ we have all to be tested as they.

Our brethren even in the church of God, while admitting in the abstract the loveliness and advantages of such an ideal life, tell us as they told Israel that it is impracticable and impossible, and many of us have to stand alone for years witnessing to the power of Christ to save His people to the uttermost and like Caleb following Him wholly, if alone. But this is the real victory of faith and the proof of our uncompromising fidelity.

Let us not therefore complain when we suffer reproach for our testimony or stand alone for God, but thank Him that He so honors us, and so stand the test that He can afterwards use us when the multitudes are glad to follow.

OCTOBER 29.

"Whatsoever ye shall ask the Father in my name, He will give it you" (John xvi. 23).

Two men go to the bank cashier, both holding in their hands a piece of paper. One is dressed in expensive style, and presents a gloved and jeweled hand; the other is a rough, unwashed workman. The first is rejected with a polite sentence, and the second receives a thousand dollars over the counter. What is the difference? The one presented a worthless name; the other handed in a note endorsed by the president of the bank. And so the most virtuous moralist will be turned away from the gates of mercy, and the vilest sinner welcomed in if he presents the name of Jesus.

What shall we give to infinite purity and righteousness? Jesus! No other gift is worthy for God to receive. And He has given Him to us for this very end, to give back as our substitute and satisfaction. And He has "testified" of this gift what He has of no other, namely, that in Him He is well pleased and all who receive Him "are accepted in the Beloved." Shall we accept the testimony that God is satisfied with His Son? Shall we be satisfied with Him?

OCTOBER 30.

"Dwell deep" (Jer. xlix. 8).

God's presence blends with every other thought and consciousness, flowing sweetly and evenly through our business plans, our social converse our heart's affections, our manual toil, our entire life, blending with all, consecrating all, and conscious through all, like the fragrance of a flower, or the presence of a friend consciously near, and yet not hindering in the least the most intense and constant preoccupation of the hands and brain. How beautiful the established habit of this unceasing communion and dependence, amid and above all thoughts and occupations! How lovely to see a dear old saint folding away his books at night and humbly saying, "Lord Jesus, things are still just the same between us," and the falling asleep in His keeping.

So let us be stayed upon Him. Let us grow into Him with all the root and fibers of our being. He will not get tired of our friendship. He will not want to put us off sometimes. Beautiful the words of the suffering saint: "He never says good-bye." He stays. So let us be stayed on Him.

OCTOBER 31.

"My grace is sufficient for thee; for My strength is made perfect in weakness" (II. Cor. xii. 9).

God allowed the crisis to close around Jacob on the night when he bowed at Peniel in supplication to bring him to the place where he could take hold of God as he never would have done; and from that narrow pass of peril Jacob came enlarged in his faith and knowledge of God, and in the power of a new and victorious life. He had to compel David, by a long and painful discipline of years, to learn the almighty power and faithfulness of his God, and to grow up into the established principles of faith and godliness, which were indispensable for his subsequent and glorious career as the king of Israel.

Nothing but the extremities in which Paul was constantly placed could ever have taught him, and taught the church through him, the full meaning of the great promise he so learned to claim, "My grace is sufficient for thee." And nothing but our trials and perils would ever have led some of us to know Him as we do, to trust Him as we have, and to draw from Him the measures of grace which our very extremities made indispensable.

NOVEMBER 1.

"We will come unto him and make our abode with him" (John xiv. 23).

This idea of trying to get a holiness of your own, and then have Christ reward you for it, is not His teaching. Oh, no; Christ is the holiness; He will bring the holiness, and come and dwell in the heart forever.

When one of our millionaires purchases a lot, with an old shanty on it, he does not fix up the old shanty, but he gets a second-hand man, if he will have it, to tear it down, and he puts a mansion in its place. It is not fixing up the house that you need, but to give Christ the vacant lot, and He will excavate below our old life and build a house where He will live forever.

Now that is what we mean when we say that Christ will be the preparation for the blessing, and make way for His own approach. It is as when a great Assyrian king used to set out on a march. He did not command the people to make a road, but he sent on his own men, and they cut down the trees and filled the broken places, and levelled the mountains. So He will, if we will let Him, be the Coming King, the Author and Finisher of our faith.

NOVEMBER 2.

"Bringing into captivity every thought to the obedience of Christ" (II. Cor. x. 5).

If we would abide in Christ we must have no confidence in self. Self-repression must be ever the prime necessity of divine fulness and efficiency. Now you know how quickly you spring to the front when any emergency arises. When something in which you are interested comes up, you say what you think under some sudden impulse, and then perhaps you have weeks of taking back your thought and taking the Lord's instead. It is only when we get out of the way of the Lord that He can use us. So, be out of self, always suspending your will about everything until you have looked at it and said: "Lord, what is your will? What is your thought about it?"

Those who thus abide in Christ have the habit of reserve and quiet; they are not rattling and reckless talkers, they will not always have an opinion about

165

everything, and they will not always know what they are going to do. There will be a deferential holding back of judgment, and walking softly with God. It is our headlong, impulsive spirit that keeps us so constantly from hearing and following the Lord.

NOVEMBER 3.

"This is my Beloved, and this is my Friend" (Song of Solomon v. 16).

He is our Friend. "Which of you shall have a friend at night?" This has deep significance through the experience of each one of us. Who has not had a friend, and more of a friend in some respects than even a father?

There are some intimacies not born of human blood that are the most intense and lasting bonds of earthly love. One by one let us count them over and recall each act and bond of love, and think of all that we may trust them for and all in which they stood by us, and then as we concentrate the whole weight of recollection and affection, let us put God in that place of confidence and think He is all that and infinitely more.

Our Friend! The one who is personally interested in us; who has set His heart upon us; who has come near to us in the tender and delicate intimacy of unspeakable fellowship; who gave us such invaluable pledges and promises; who has done so much for us, and who is ever ready to take any trouble or go to any expense to aid us--to Him we are coming in prayer, our Heavenly Friend.

NOVEMBER 4.

"Hath the Lord as great delight in burnt offerings as in obeying the voice of the Lord?" (I. Sam. xv. 22).

Many a soul prays for sanctification, but fails to enter into the blessing because he does not intelligently understand and believingly accept God's appointed means by Jesus Christ and the indwelling of the Spirit. Many a prayer for the salvation of others is hindered because the very friend takes the wrong course to bring about the answer, and resorts to means which are wholly fitted to defeat his worthy object.

We know many a wife who is pleading for her husband's soul, and hoping to win him by avoiding anything that may offend him, and yielding to all his worldly tastes in the vain hope of attracting him to Christ. Far more effective would be an attitude of fidelity to God and fearless testimony to Him, such as God could bless.

Many a congregation wonders why it is so poor and struggling. It may be found that its financial methods are wholly unscriptural and often unworthy of ordinary self-respect.

When we ask God for any blessing, we must allow Him to direct the steps which are to bring the answer.

NOVEMBER 5.

"I in them, and Thou in Me" (John xvii. 23).

If we would be enlarged to the full measure of God's purpose, let us endeavor to realize something of our own capacities for His filling.

We little know the size of a human soul and spirit. Never, until He renews, cleanses and enters the heart can we have any adequate conception of the possibilities of the being whom God made in His very image, and whom He now renews after the pattern of the Lord Jesus Himself.

We know, however, that God has made the human soul to be His temple and abode, and that He knows how to make the house that can hold His infinite fulness. We know something of this as all our nature quickens into spring tide life at the coming of the Holy Spirit, and as from time to time new baptisms awaken the dormant powers and susceptibilities that we did not know we possessed.

Oh, let us give Him the right to make the best of us, and, with wonder filled, we shall some day behold the glorious temple which He has reared, and shall say, "Lord, what is man that Thou hast set Thine heart upon Him?"

NOVEMBER 6.

"Bless the Lord, O, my soul" (Ps. ciii. 1).

Bless the Lord, O my soul; and all that is within me be stirred up to magnify His holy name. "Bless the Lord, O my soul, and forget not all His benefits; who forgiveth all thine iniquities; who healeth all thy diseases; who redeemeth thy life from destruction; who crowneth thee with lovingkindness and tender mercies; who satisfieth thy mouth with good things, so that thy youth is renewed like the eagle's." Who so well can sing this thanksgiving song as we, rejoicing as most of us do, we trust, in this full salvation, and praising God for the glorious health of a risen Lord and a continual youth?

167

This psalm and its opening verses is in the very center of the Scriptures by an exact count of letters and verses. So let it stand in our lives, as we look backward and forward and upward in grateful thanksgiving as we sing in its closing strains, "Bless the Lord, O my soul, and all that is within me, bless His holy name." Lord, center my heart in Thee and in the spirit of love and praise.

NOVEMBER 7.

"I will strengthen thee; yea, I will help thee; yea, I will uphold thee" (Isa. xli. 10).

God has three ways of helping us: First, He says, "I will strengthen thee"; that is, I will make you a little stronger yourself. And secondly, "I will help thee"; that is, I will add My strength to your strength, but you shall lead and I will help you. But thirdly, when you are ready, "I will uphold thee with the right hand of My righteousness"; that is, I will lift you up bodily and carry you altogether, and it will neither be your strength or My help, but My complete upholding. Hence it must be quite true, that when we come to the end of our strength, we come to the beginning of His, and that in Him the weakest are the strongest, and the most helpless the most helped. "He giveth power to the faint," but to "them that have no might" at all "He gives more strength," and His word forever is, "My grace is sufficient for thee." The answer is a paradox of contradictions, and yet the most practical truths, "Most gladly, therefore, will I glory in my infirmities, that the power of Christ may rest upon me; for when I am weak, then am I strong."

NOVEMBER 8.

"For the law of the Spirit of life in Christ Jesus hath made me free" (Rom. viii. 2).

There is a natural law of sin and sickness, and if we just let ourselves go and sink into the trend of circumstances we shall go down and sink under the power of the tempter. But there is another law of spiritual life and of physical life in Christ Jesus to which we can rise and through which we can counterpoise and overcome the other law that bears us down. But to do this requires real spiritual energy and fixed purpose and a settled posture and habit of faith. It is just the same when we bind the power in our factory. We must turn the belt on and keep it on. The power is there, but we must keep the connection and while we do so the law of this higher power will work and all the machinery will be in operation.

168

There is a spiritual law of choosing, believing, abiding and holding steady in our walk with God which is essential to the working of the Holy Ghost either in our sanctification or healing.

There is a word that saves the soul,

"I will trust";

It makes the sick and suffering whole.

"I will trust."

NOVEMBER 9.

"Because I live ye shall live also" (John xiv. 19).

After having become adjusted to our Living Head and the source of our life, now our business is to abide, absorb and grow, leaning on His strength, drinking in His life, feeding on Him as the Living Bread, and drawing all of our resources from Him in continual dependence and communion. The Holy Spirit will be the great Teacher and Minister in this blessed process. He will take of the things of Christ and show them unto us, and He will impart them through all the channels and functions of our spiritual organism. As we yield ourselves to Him He will breathe His own prayer of communion, drawing out our hearts in longings and hungerings, which are the pledge of their own fulfilment, calling us apart in silent and wordless prayer and opening every pore, organ, sense and sensibility of our spiritual being to take in His life. As the lungs absorb the oxygen of the atmosphere, as the senses breathe in the sweet odors of the garden, so the heart instinctively receives and rejoices in the affection and fellowship of the beloved One by our side. Thus we become like a tree planted by the rivers of waters.

NOVEMBER 10.

"But prayer was made without ceasing, of the church unto God for him" (Acts xii. 5).

But prayer is the link that connects us with God. This is the bridge that spans every gulf and bears us over every abyss of danger or of need. How significant the picture of the apostolic church: Peter in prison, the Jews triumphant, Herod supreme, the arena of martyrdom awaiting the dawning of the morning to drink up the apostle's blood,--everything else against it. "But prayer was made unto God without ceasing." And what the sequel? The prison open,--the apostle free,--

169

the Jews baffled,--the wicked king eaten of worms, a spectacle of hideous retribution, and the Word of God rolling on in greater victory.

Do we know the power of our supernatural weapon? Do we dare to use it with the authority of a faith that commands as well as asks? God baptize us with holy audacity and Divine confidence. He is not wanting great men, but He is wanting men that will dare to prove the greatness of their God.

But God! But prayer!

NOVEMBER 11.

"Reckon yourselves dead, indeed" (Rom. vi. 11).

Our life from the dead is to be followed up by the habit and attitude henceforth which is the logical outcome of all this. "Reckon yourselves _dead indeed_, unto sin, but _alive unto God_ through Jesus Christ, and yield yourselves unto God," not to die over again every day, "_but, as those who are alive from the dead_, and your members as instruments of righteousness unto God."

Further His resurrection life is given to fit us for "the fellowship of His sufferings and to be made conformable unto His death."

It is intended to enable us to toil and suffer with rejoicing and victory. We "mount up with wings as eagles," that we may come back to "run and not be weary, to walk and not faint."

But let us not mistake the sufferings. They do not mean _our_ sufferings, but His. They are not our struggles after holiness, our sicknesses and pains, but those higher sufferings which, with Him, we bear for others, and for a suffering church and a dying world. May God help us, henceforth, never to have another sorrow for ourselves, and put us at leisure, in the power of His resurrection, to bear His burdens and drink His cup.

NOVEMBER 12.

"The earnest of the Spirit in our hearts" (II. Cor. i. 22).

Life in earnest. What a rare, what a glorious spectacle! We see it in the Son of God, we see it in His apostle, we see it in every noble, consecrated and truly successful life. Without it there may be a thousand good things, but they lack the golden thread that binds them all into a chain of power and permanence. They are like a lot of costly and beautiful beads on a broken string, that fall into confusion, and are lost in the end for want of the bond that alone could bind them into a life of consistent and lasting power. O for the baptism of fire! O for "THE EARNEST, THE SPIRIT!" O for lives that have but one thing to do or care for! O for the depth and everlasting strength of the heart of Christ within our breast, to love, to sacrifice, to realize, to persevere, to live and die like Him!

We are going forth with a trust so sacred,
And a truth so divine and deep,
With a message clear and a work so glorious,
And a charge--such a charge--to keep.
Let it be your greatest joy, my brother,
That the Lord can count on you;
And if all besides should fail and falter,
To your trust be always true.

NOVEMBER 13.

"Delight thyself in the Lord" (Ps. xxxvii. 4).

Daniel's heart was filled with God's love for His work and kingdom and his prayers were the mightiest forces of his time, through which God gave to him the restoration of Israel to their own land, and the acknowledgment by the rulers of the world of the God of whom he testified and for whom he lived.

There is a beautiful promise in the thirty-seventh Psalm, "Delight thyself in the Lord, and He will give thee the desires of thine heart," which it is, perhaps, legitimate to translate, that not only does it mean the fulfilment of our desires, but even the inspiration of our desires, the inbreathing of His thoughts into us, so that our prayers shall be in accord with His will and so shall bring back to us the unfailing answer of His mighty providence.

Teach me Thy thoughts, O God!
Think Thou, Thyself, in me,
Then shall I only always think
Thine own thoughts after Thee.

Teach me Thy thoughts, O God!
Show me Thy plan divine:
Save me from all my plans and works,
And lead me into Thine.

NOVEMBER 14.

171

"The things which are seen are temporal" (II. Cor. iv. 18).

How strong is the snare of the things that are seen, and how necessary for God to keep us in the things that are unseen! If Peter is to walk on the water, he must walk; if he is going to swim, he must swim, but he cannot do both. If the bird is going to fly it must keep away from the fences and the trees, and trust to its buoyant wings. But if it tries to keep within easy reach of the ground, it will make poor work of flying.

God had to bring Abraham to the end of his own strength, and to let him see that in his own body he could do nothing. He had to consider his own body as good as dead, and then take God for the whole work, and when he looked away from himself, and trusted God alone, then He became fully persuaded that what He had promised, He was able also to perform.

This is what God is teaching us, and He has to keep away encouraging results until we learn to trust without them, and then He loves to make His word real in fact as well as faith.

Let us look only to Him to-day to do all things as He shall choose and in the way He shall choose.

NOVEMBER 15.

"Oh, man of desires" (margin) (Dan. x. 11).

This was the divine character given to Daniel of old. It is translated in our version, "O man, greatly beloved." But it literally means "O man of desires!" This is a necessary element in all spiritual forces. It is one of the secrets of effectual prayer, "What things soever ye desire, when ye pray, believe that ye receive them." The element of strong desire gives momentum to our purposes and prayers. Indifference is an unwholesome condition; indolence and apathy are offensive both to God and nature.

And so in our spiritual life, God often has to wake us up by the presence of trying circumstances, and push us into new places of trust by forces that we must subdue, or sink beneath their power. There is no factor in prayer more effectual than love. If we are intensely interested in an object, or an individual, our petitions become like living forces, and not only convey their wants to God, but in some sense convey God's help back to them.

172

May God fill us to-day with the heart of Christ that we may glow with the Divine fire of holy desire.

NOVEMBER 16.

"Watch therefore, for ye know neither the day" (Matt. xxv. 13).

Jesus illustrates the unexpectedness of His coming by the figure of a thief entering a house when the master was not there. Life, like the old Jewish night, may be divided into three watches, youth, maturity, old age. The summons to meet God may come to us in either of these watches. A writer tells us of his experience with a camping party, of which he was a member, and which, he tells us, always arranged to have watches at night. "We became especially careful after what I am about to narrate happened. During the first night, from sunset to sunrise, we had in turn carefully guarded our camp. But when the next night came, so impressed were we with the orderly character of the neighborhood, that we concluded that no guard was needed until bedtime. Within our main tent the evening was spent in story-telling, singing and general amusement. When the hour to retire arrived, it was discovered that our other tents had been robbed and everything of value stolen. The work was done before we thought a guard necessary." It is never too soon to begin watching against sin.

NOVEMBER 17.

"The ark of the covenant of the Lord went before them" (Num. x. 33).

God does give us impressions but not that we should act on them as impressions. If the impression be from God, He will Himself give sufficient evidence to establish it beyond the possibility of a doubt.

How beautifully we read, in the story of Jeremiah, of the impression that came to him respecting the purchase of the field of Anathoth, but Jeremiah did not act upon this impression until after the following day, when his uncle's son came to him and brought him external evidence by making a proposal for the purchase. Then Jeremiah said: "I knew this was the word of the Lord."

He waited until God seconded the impression by a providence, and then he acted in full view of the open facts, which could bring conviction unto others as well as himself.

God wants us to act according to His mind.

173

We are not to ignore the Shepherd's personal voice, but like Paul and his companions at Troas, we are to listen to all the voices that speak, and "gather" from all the circumstances, as they did, the full mind of the Lord.

NOVEMBER 18.

"And He that sat upon the throne said, It is done" (Rev. xxi. 5, 6).

Great is the difference between action and transaction. We may be constantly acting without accomplishing anything, but a transaction is action that passes beyond the point of return, and becomes a permanent committal. Salvation is a transaction between the soul and Christ in which the matter passes beyond recall. Sanctification is a great transaction in which we are utterly surrendered, irrevocably consecrated and wholly committed to the Holy Ghost, and then He comes and seals the transaction and undertakes the work. Our covenant for our Lord's healing should be just as explicit, definite and irrevocable. And so of the covenants to which God is leading His children from time to time in regard to other matters of obedience and service. God grant that during this hallowed day many a consecrated life may be able to say with new significance and permanence, "'Tis done, the great transaction's done."

For the living Vine is Jesus,
In whose fulness we may hide;
And find our life and fruitfulness
As we in Him abide.

NOVEMBER 19.

"We would see Jesus" (John xii. 21).

When any great blessing is awaiting us, the devil is sure to try and make it so disagreeable to us that we shall miss it. It is a good thing to know him as a liar, and remember, when he is trying to prejudice us strongly against any cause, that very likely the greatest blessing of our life lies there. Spurgeon once said that the best evidence that God was on our side is the devil's growl, and we are generally pretty safe in following a thing according to Satan's dislike for it. Beloved, take care, lest in the very line where your prejudices are setting you off from God's people and God's truth, you are missing the treasures of your life. Take the treasures of heaven no matter how they come to you, even if it be as earthly

174

treasures generally are, like the kernel inside the rough shell, or the gem in the bosom of the hard rock.

I have seen Jesus and my heart is dead to all beside,

I have seen Jesus, and my wants are all, in Him, supplied.

I have seen Jesus, and my heart, at last, is satisfied,

Since I've seen Jesus.

NOVEMBER 20.

"The disciple whom Jesus loved leaned on His breast" (John xxi. 20).

An American gentleman once visited the saintly Albert Bengel. He was very desirous to hear him pray. So one night he lingered at his door, hoping to overhear his closing devotions. The rooms were adjoining and the doors ajar. The good man finished his studies, closed his books, knelt down for a moment and simply said: "Dear Lord Jesus, things are still the same between us," and then sweetly fell asleep. So close was his communion with his Lord that labor did not interrupt it, and prayer was not necessary to renew it. It was a ceaseless, almost unconscious presence, like the fragrance of the summer garden, or the presence of some dear one by our side whose presence we somehow feel, even though the busy hours pass by and not a word is exchanged.

"O blessed fellowship, divine,

O joy, supremely sweet,

Companionship with Jesus here,

Makes life with joy replete;

O wondrous grace, O joy sublime,

I've Jesus with me all the time."

NOVEMBER 21.

"Consider the lilies how they grow" (Matt. vi. 28).

It is said that a little fellow was found one day by his mother, standing by a tall sunflower, with his feet stuck in the ground. When asked by her, "What in the world are you doing there?" he naively answered, "Why, I am trying to grow to be a man."

His mother laughed heartily at the idea of his getting planted in the ground in order to grow, like the sunflower, and then, patting him gently on the head, "Why, Harry, that is not the way to grow. You can never grow bigger by trying.

175

Just come right in, and eat lots of good food, and have plenty of play, and you will soon grow to be a man without trying so hard."

Well, Harry's mother was right. Mrs. H. W. Smith never said a sweeter thing than when she answered the question--"How do the lilies grow?" by simply adding, "They grow without trying."

Our sweetest spiritual life is the life of self-unconsciousness through which we become so united to Christ, and live continually on His life, nourished, fed and constantly filled with His Spirit and presence and all the fulness of His imparted life.

NOVEMBER 22.

"Cast the beam out of thine own eye" (Matt. vii. 5).

Greater than the fault you condemn and criticise is the sin of criticism and condemnation. There is no place we need such grace as in dealing with an erring one. A lady once called on us on her way to give an erring sister a piece of her mind. We advised her to wait until she could love her a little more. Only He who loved sinners well enough to die for them can deal with the erring. We never see all the heart. He does, and He can convict without condemning, and reprove without discouraging. Oh, for more of the heart of Christ! Take care, brother, how you speak of another's fault. Ere you know, you may be in the same or deeper condemnation. Very significantly does the Master say that the man that sees a mote in his brother's eye, usually has a rafter in his own eye! One of the two unpardonable sins of the Bible is unforgiving lovelessness.

"Give me a heart like Thine,

Give me a heart like Thine,

By Thy wonderful power,

By Thy grace every hour,

Give me a heart like Thine."

NOVEMBER 23.

"It is high time to awake out of sleep" (Rom. xiii. 11).

One of the greatest enemies to faith is indolence. It is much easier to lie and suffer than to rise and overcome; much easier to go to sleep on a snowbank and never wake again, than to rouse one's self and shake off the lethargy and

176

overcome the stupor. Faith is an energetic art; prayer is intense labor; the effectual working prayer of the righteous man availeth much.

Satan tries to put us to sleep, as he did the disciples in the garden; but let us not sleep as do others, but let us wake and be sober, continuing in prayer and watching therein with all perseverance, stirring up ourselves to take hold of His strength, "not slothful, but followers of them, who, through patience, inherit the promise." It is the wind that carries the ship across the waves; but the wind is powerless unless the hand of the boatman is held firmly upon the rudder, and that rudder is set hard against the wind. In like manner we hold the rudder, God fills the sails. It is not the rudder that carries the ship; but it is the rudder which catches the wind that carries the ship, so God keeps us in perfect peace while we are stayed upon Him.

NOVEMBER 24.

"I can do all things through Christ" (Phil. iv. 13).

A dear sister said one day: "I have so much work to do that I have not time to get strength to do it by waiting on the Lord." Surely that was making bricks without straw, and even if it was the name of the Lord and the church, it was the devil's bondage. God sends not His servants on their own charges; but "He is able to make all grace abound towards us, that we, always having all sufficiency in all things, may abound unto every good work." The old story of the chieftain, fleeing from his foes and almost overtaken, but stopping in the midst of his flight to get a shoe upon his horse that he might fly more successfully is a true type and lesson for Christian workers.

The old Latin motto _festina lente_, "make haste slowly," has a great lesson for us. The more work we have to do, the more frequently we have to drop our head upon our desk and wait a little for heavenly aid and love, and then press on with new strength. One hour baptized in the love of the Holy Ghost is worth ten battling against wind and tide without the heavenly life.

NOVEMBER 25.

"Judge nothing before the time, until the Lord come" (I. Cor. iv. 5).

Nothing will more effectually arrest the working of the Spirit in the heart than the spirit of criticism. At the end of a meeting a young minister came forward and told us of the great blessing he had received that afternoon, and the baptism of

177

the Holy Spirit that had come into his heart and being, setting him free from the bondage of years. And then he added, "It all came through your answer to that question, 'Will a criticizing spirit hinder the Holy Ghost from filling the heart?' "

As the question was asked and answered, he said, "I was sitting in the church criticizing a good deal that was going on, objecting to this thing and to that thing, finding fault with the expressions, and praises and testimonies, and feeling thoroughly unhappy. The Lord brought the answer home to my heart and convicted me of my sin, and there and then I laid it down and began to see the good instead of the evil. Blessing fell upon me and my soul was filled with joy and praise, and I saw where my error lay, that for years I had been trying to see the truth with my head instead of my heart."

NOVEMBER 26.

"He purgeth it that it may bring forth more fruit" (John xv. 2).

One day we passed a garden. The gardener had finished his pruning, and the wounds of the knife and saw were beginning to heal, while the warm April sun was gently nourishing the stricken plant into fresh life and energy. We thought as we looked at that plant how cruel it would be to begin next week and cut it down again. It would bleed to death. Now, the gardener's business is to revive and nourish into life. Its business is not to die, but to live. So, we thought, it is with the discipline of the soul. It, too, has its dying hour; but it must not be always dying. Rather reckon ourselves to be dead indeed unto sin and alive unto God through Jesus Christ our Lord Everlasting.

Breathe Thine own breath through all my mortal frame,

Help me Thy resurrection life to claim,

Which, 'mid all changes, still abides the same,

And lead me in the way Everlasting.

Give me the heavenly foretaste here, I pray;

Let faith foredate the everlasting day,

And walking in its glory all the way,

O, lead me in the way Everlasting!

NOVEMBER 27.

"And the remnant of the oil ... shall pour upon the head" (Lev. xiv. 18).

In the account of the healing of the Hebrew leper there is a beautiful picture of the touching of his ears, hands and feet, with the redeeming blood and the consecrating oil, as a sign that his powers of understanding, service, and conduct were set apart to God, and divinely endued for the Master's work and will.

But after all this, we are significantly told that "the rest of the oil" was to be poured upon his head.

The former anointing was from the oil in the hand of the priest, but the latter was to be from the log, or vessel of oil itself. It was to be literally emptied over him, until he was bathed with all its contents.

It is a figure of the large and boundless baptism of the Holy Ghost. It speaks of something more even than the ordinary experiences of the consecrated Christian. It tells of the abundant and redundant supply which God has for us out of His illimitable fulness.

Have we received "the rest oil"? Are we _filled_ with the Spirit, and letting the overflow bless others?

NOVEMBER 28.

"Without Me ye can do nothing" (John xv. 5).

How much can I do for Christ? We are accustomed to say.--As much as I can. Have we ever thought we can do more than we can?

This thought was lately suggested by the remarks of a Christian friend, who told how God had laid it upon her heart to do something for His cause which was beyond her power, and when she dared to obey Him, He gave her the assurance of His power and resources, and so marvelously met her faith that she was enabled to do more than she could otherwise, and accomplish her heart's desire, and see a work fulfilled to which her resources were unequal.

The apostle says, "I can do all things through Christ, who is my strength," and yet He says we are not able to think anything, as of ourselves.

Oh, blessed insufficiency! Oh, blessed All-Sufficiency! Oh, blessed nothingness, which brings us all things! Oh, blessed faith, whose rich dowry is, "All things are possible to him that believeth"!

O to be found of Him in peace,

Spotless and free from blame.

NOVEMBER 29.

179

"Could ye not watch with Me one hour?" (Matt. xxvi. 40.)

A young lady whose parents had died while she was an infant, had been kindly cared for by a dear friend of the family. Before she was old enough to know him, he went to Europe. Regularly he wrote to her through all his years of absence, and never failed to send her money for all her wants. Finally word came that during a certain week he would return and visit her. He did not fix the day or the hour. She received several invitations to take pleasant trips with her friends during that week. One of these was of so pleasant a nature that she could not resist accepting it. During her trip, he came, inquired as to her absence, and left. Returning she found this note: "My life has been a struggle for you, might you not have waited one week for me?" More she never heard, and her life of plenty became one of want. Jesus has not fixed the day or hour of His return, but He has said, "Watch," and should He come to-day, would He find us absorbed in thoughtless dissipation? May we be found each day, in the expectant attitude of those watching for a loved one.

NOVEMBER 30.

"In lowliness of mind let each esteem other better than themselves" (Phil. ii. 3).

When the apostle speaks of "the deep things of God," he means more than deep spiritual truth. There must be something before this. There must be a deep soil and a thorough foundation.

Very much of our spiritual teaching fails, because the people to whom we give it are so shallow. Their deeper nature has never been stirred.

The beatitudes begin at the bottom of things, the poor in spirit, the mourners, and the hungry hearts. Suffering is essential to profound spiritual life. We need not go to a monastery or a leper hospital to find it. The first real opportunity for unselfishness will bring into your life the anguish of crucifixion, unless you are born of some different race from Adam's.

It is because men and women have not faced this that they know so little of suffering and death. We must have deep convictions. Truth must be to us a necessity, and principle a part of our very being. Lord, make me poor in spirit. Lord help me to be even as Thou wert when on earth, always the lowest, and therefore "highly exalted."

180

DECEMBER 1.

"As He is, so are we in this world" (I. John iv. 17).

Jesus will come into the surrendered heart and unite Himself with it, impart to it His own life and being and become anew from day to day, the supply of its spiritual needs and the substitute for its helplessness.

Our part is simply to yield ourselves fully recognizing our own worthlessness and then take Jesus Himself to live in us and be, moment by moment, our strength, purity and victory.

One in His death on the tree,
One as He rose from the dead;
I from the curse am as free
E'en as my glorious Head.

One in His merits I stand,
One as I Pray in His name,
All that His worth can demand
I may with confidence claim.

One on the Throne by His side,
One in His Sonship divine,
One as the Bridegroom and Bride,
One as the Branch and the Vine.

All that He has shall be mine,
All that He is I shall be;
Robed in His glory divine,
I shall be even as He.

DECEMBER 2.

"Looking diligently lest any man fail" (Heb. xii. 15).

It is not losing all, but coming short we are to fear. We may not lose our souls, but we may lose something more precious than life--His full approval, His highest choice, and our incorruptible and star-gemmed crown. It is the one degree more that counts, and makes all the difference between hot water--powerless in the boiler--and steam--all alive with power, and bearing its precious freight across the continent.

181

I want, in this short life of mine,
As much as can be pressed
Of service true for God and man,
Help me to be my best.

I want to stand when Christ appears
And hear my name confessed
Numbered among the hidden ones,
His holiest and best.

I want, among the victor throng,
To have my name confessed;
And hear my Master say at last,
Well done, you did your best.

Give me, O Lord, Thy highest choice;
Let others take the rest:
Their good things have no charm for me,
For I have got Thy best.

DECEMBER 3.

Thy thoughts are very deep (Ps. xcii. 5).

When a Roman soldier was told by his guide that if he insisted on taking a certain journey it would probably be fatal he answered, "It is necessary for me to go, it is not necessary for me to live." That was depth. When we are convicted like that we shall come to something.

The shallow nature lives in its impulses, its impressions, its intuitions, its instincts, and very largely in its surroundings. The profound character looks beyond all these and moves steadily on, sailing past all the storms and clouds into the clear sunshine which is always on the other side, and waiting for the afterwards which always brings the reversion of sorrow and seeming defeat and failure.

When God has deepened us, then He can give us His deeper truths, His profoundest secrets, and His mightier trusts.

Lord, lead me into the depths of Thy life and save me from a shallow experience.

On to broader fields of holy vision;

On to loftier heights of faith and love;

Onward, upward, apprehending wholly,

All for which He calls thee from above.

DECEMBER 4.

"From me is thy fruit found" (Hos. xiv. 8).

Nothing keeps us from advancement more than ruts and drifts, and wheel-tracks into which our chariots roll and then move on in the narrow line with unchanging monotony, currents in life's stream on which we are borne in the old direction until the law of habit almost makes advance impossible. The true remedy for this is to commence at nothing; taking Christ afresh to be the Alpha and Omega for a deeper, higher, Divine experience, waiting even for His conception of thought, desire, prayer, and afraid lest our highest thought should be below His great plan of wisdom and love.

O Comforter gentle and tender,

O holy and heavenly Dove,

We're yielding our heart in surrender,

We're waiting Thy fulness to prove.

O come as the heart-searching fire,

O come as the sin-cleansing flood;

Consume us with holy desire,

And fill with the fulness of God.

Anoint us with gladness and healing;

Baptize us with power from on high;

O come with filling and sealing

While low at the Thy footstool we lie.

DECEMBER 5.

"With a perfect heart to make David King" (I. Chron. xii. 38).

"What is the supreme purpose of our life? They were all of one heart to make David king." Is this our purpose, to prepare the Bride, to prepare the world, to prepare His way? Does it dwarf and dim all other ambitions, all other cares? Does it fill and satisfy every capacity, every power, every desire? Does it absorb every moment, every energy, every resource? Does it give direction and tone to every plan and work of life? Does it decide for us the education of our children, the investment of our means, the friendships and associations of life, the whole activity, interest and outlook of our being? Are we in it, spirit, soul and body, all we are, all we do, all we hope for--OF ONE HEART TO MAKE JESUS KING?

We're going forth united
With loyal heart and hand,
To bear His royal banner
Aboard o'er every land.

From every tribe and nation
We'll haste His Bride to bring.
And Oh, with what glad welcome
We'll make our Jesus King.

DECEMBER 6.

"Humble yourselves therefore under the mighty hand of God, that He may exalt you" (I. Peter v. 6).

Opposition is essential to a true equilibrium of forces. The centripetal and centrifugal forces acting in opposition to each other keep our planet in her orbit. The one propelling, and the other repelling, so act and react, that instead of sweeping off into space in a pathway of desolation and destruction, she pursues her even orbit around her solar center.

So God guides our lives. It is not enough to have an impelling force--we need just as much a repelling force, and so He holds us back by the testing ordeals of life, by the pressure of temptation and trial, by the things that seem to be against us, but really are furthering our way and stablishing our goings. Let us thank Him for both, let us take the weights as well as the wings, and thus divinely impelled, let us press on with faith and patience in our high and heavenly calling.

Lord, help me to learn from all that comes to me this day Thy highest will.

Lord, help me to-day to sink under Thy blessed hand, that Thou mayest have Thy way and will with me.

DECEMBER 7.

"Abide with us; for it is toward evening" (Luke xxiv. 29).

In His last messages to the disciples in the 14th and 15th chapters of John, the Lord Jesus clearly teaches us that the very essence of the highest holiness is, "Abide in Me, and I in you, for without Me ye can do nothing."

The very purpose of the Holy Ghost whom He promised was to reveal Him, that at "that day, ye shall know that I am in the Father, and ye in Me, and I in you," and the closing echo of His intercessory prayer was embraced in these three small but infinite words, "I in them."

Is it for me to be cleansed by His power
From the pollution of sin?
Is it for me to be kept every hour
By His abiding within?

Is it for me to be perfectly whole
Thro' His anointing divine;
Claiming in body, and spirit, and soul,
All of His fulness as mine?

Wonderful promise so full and so free,
Wonderful Saviour, Oh, how can it be,
Cleansing and pardon and mercy for me?
Yes, it's for me, for me.

DECEMBER 8.

"Is there no balm in Gilead; is there no physician there?" (Jer. viii. 22).

Divine healing is just divine life. It is the headship of Christ over the body. It is the life of Christ in the frame. It is the union of our members with the very body of Christ and the inflowing life of Christ in our living members. It is as real as His risen and glorified body. It is as reasonable as the fact that He was raised from the dead and is a living man with a true body and a rational soul to-day, at God's right hand. That living Christ belongs to us in all His attributes and powers. We are members of His body, His flesh and His bones, and if we can only believe and receive it, we may live upon the very life of the Son of God.

Lord, help me to know the "Lord for the body and the body for the Lord."

There is healing in the promise,
There is healing in the blood,

185

There is strength for all our weakness

In the risen Son of God.

And the feeblest of His children,

All His glorious life may share;

He has healing balm in Gilead,

He's the Great Physician there.

DECEMBER 9.

"Launch out into the deep" (Luke v. 4).

One of the special marks of the Holy Ghost in the Apostolic Church was the spirit Of boldness. One of the most essential qualities of the faith that is to attempt great things for God and expect great things from God, is holy audacity. Where we are dealing with a supernatural Being, and taking from Him things that are humanly impossible, it is easier to take much than little; it is easier to stand in a place of audacious trust than in a place of cautious, timid clinging to the shore. Like wise seamen in the life of faith, let us launch out into the deep, and find that all things are possible with God, and all things are possible unto him that believeth.

Let us to-day attempt great things for God, take His faith and believe for them and His strength to accomplish them.

The mercy of God is an ocean divine,

A boundless and fathomless flood;

Launch out in the deep, cut away the shore-line,

And be lost in the fulness of God.

Oh, let us launch out in this ocean so broad,

Where the floods of salvation o'erflow,

Oh, let us be lost in the mercy of God,

Till the depth of His fulness we know.

DECEMBER 10.

"According to the measure of the rule which God hath distributed" (II. Cor. x. 13).

According to thy faith be it unto thee was Christ's great law of healing and blessing in His earthly ministry. This was what He meant when He said, "With what measure ye mete it shall be measured to you again." These mighty measures

186

are limited by the the measures that we bring. God deals out His heavenly treasures to us in these glorious vessels, but each of us must bring our drinking cup, and according to its measure we shall be filled.

But even the measure of our faith may be a Divine one. Thank God, the little cup has become enlarged through the grace of Jesus, until from its bottom there flows a pipe into the great ocean, and if that connection is kept open we shall find that our cup is as large as the ocean and never can be drained to the bottom. For He has said to us, "Have the faith of God," and surely this is an illimitable measure.

Let us claim the mighty promise,
Let us light the torches dim;
Let us join the glorious chorus,
Nothing is too hard for Him.

DECEMBER 11.

"I pray not for the world, but for them" (John xvii. 9).

How often we say we would like to get some strong spirit to pray for us, and feel so helped when we think they are carrying us in their faith. But there is One whose prayers never fail to be fulfilled and who is more willing to give them to us than any human friend. His one business at God's right hand is to make intercession for His people, and we are simply coming in the line of His own appointment and His own definite promise and provision, when we lay our burdens upon Him and claim His advocacy without doubt or fear. "Seeing then that we have a great High Priest that is passed into the heavens, Jesus, the Son of God, let us come boldly to the throne of grace that we may find help in time of need."

Like a golden censer glowing,
Filled with burning odors rare,
All my heart is upward flowing,
In a cloud of ceaseless prayer.

O'er the heavenly altar bending,
Jesus interceding stands,
All our prayers to heaven ascending,
Reach the Father through His hands.

187

DECEMBER 12.

"To abide in the flesh is more needful for you, and having this confidence, I know that I shall abide" (Phil. i. 24, 25).

One of the most blessed things about divine healing is that the strength it brings is holy strength, and finds its natural and congenial outflow in holy acts and exercises.

Mere natural strength seeks its gratification in natural pleasures and activities, but the strength of Christ leads us to do as Christ would do, and to seek our congenial employment in His holy service.

The life of Christ in a human body saves it from a thousand temptations to self-indulgence and sin, and not only gives us strength for higher service, but also a desire for it, and puts into it a zest and spring which gives it double power.

Lord, help us to-day to claim Thy life and then give it for the help of others.

Have you found the branch of healing?

Pass it on.

Have you felt the Spirit's sealing,

Pass it on.

'Twas for this His mercy sought you,

And to all His fulness brought you,

By the precious blood that bought you,

Pass it on.

DECEMBER 13.

"He that abideth in Me and I in him the same bringeth forth much fruit for apart from Me ye can do nothing" (John xv. 5).

So familiar are the vine and the branches, it is not necessary to explain; only the branches and the vine are one. The vine does not say, I am the central trunk running up and you are the little branches; but I am the whole thing, and you are the whole thing. He counts us partakers of His nature. "Apart from Me ye can do nothing." The husband and the wife, and many more figures contribute to this marvelous Christ teaching, which has no parallel, no precedent in any other teaching under the sun; that Christ is the life of His people, and that we are absolutely linked with and dependent upon Him. All other systems teach how

188

much man is and may become. Christianity shows how a man must lose all he is if he would come into full unity with Christ in His life.

Lord, help me this day to abide in Thee.

Oh! what a wonderful place
Jesus has given to me!
Saved by His glorious grace,
I may be even as He.

DECEMBER 14.

"Instead of the thorn shall come up the fir tree" (Isa. lv. 13).

Difficulties and obstacles are God's challenges to faith. When hindrances confront us in the path of duty we are to recognize them as vessels for faith to fill with the fulness and all-sufficiency of Jesus, and as we go forward, simply and fully trusting Him, we may be tested, we may have to wait and let patience have her perfect work, but we shall surely find at last the stone rolled away, and the Lord waiting to render unto us double for our time of testing, and fulfil the promise, "Instead of the thorn shall come up the fir tree, instead of the brier the myrtle tree, and it shall be to the Lord for an everlasting sign that shall not be cut off."

Oft there comes a wondrous message
When my hopes are growing dim;
I can hear it through the darkness,
Like some sweet and far-off hymn.
Nothing is too hard for Jesus,
No man can work like Him.

When my way is closed in darkness
And my foes are fierce and grim,
Still it sings above the conflict
Like some glad, victorious hymn:
Nothing is too hard for Jesus,
No man can work like Him.

DECEMBER 15.

"When my heart is overwhelmed lead me to the Rock that is higher than I" (Ps. lxi. 2).

189

The end of self is the beginning of God. "When the tale of bricks is doubled then comes Moses." That is the old Hebrew way of putting it. "Man's extremity is God's opportunity." That is the proverbial expression of it. "When my heart is overwhelmed, lead me to the rock that is higher than I." That is David's way of expressing it. "We have no might against this company, neither know we what to do." No might, no light--"but our eyes are upon Thee," that was Jehoshaphat's experience of it. "Mine eyes fail with looking upward. I am oppressed, Lord, undertake for me."

"When I had great trouble I always went to God and was wondrously carried through; but in my little trials I used to try to manage them myself, and often most signally failed." So Miss Havergal has expressed the experience of many a Christian. God wants us "at our wit's end," and then He will show His wisdom, love and power. How often we ask God to help, and then begin to count up the human probabilities! God's very blessings become a hindrance to us if we look from Him to them.

DECEMBER 16.

"I will restore to you the years that the locust hath eaten, the canker worm and the caterpillar and the palmer worm, my great army, which I sent among you" (Joel ii. 25).

A friend said to me once: "I have got to reap what I sowed, for God has said: 'Whatsoever a man soweth, that shall he also reap.' Then why don't you apply this in the spiritual world, and compel the sinner to pay the penalty of his sins?"

Christ has borne this penalty, and the same Christ has borne the natural penalties, too, and delivered us out of condemnation in every sense. Physical sufferings come to us, but not under the law of retribution, but only as a Divine discipline. Every penalty has been fulfilled by Christ and every law satisfied, and so far as we can have risen with Him into the plane of spiritual and eternal life, we are lifted above the mere realm of law, and we enter into the full effects of His complete satisfaction of every claim against us. So it is true that even the wreck that sin has brought upon our physical and temporal life is removed by His great atonement, and the promise is made real to us, "I will restore to you the years that the locust hath eaten."

DECEMBER 17.

190

"Be careful for nothing" (Phil. iv. 6).

What is the way to lay your burden down? "Take My yoke upon you, and learn of Me; for I am meek and and lowly of heart, and ye shall find rest unto your souls."

"For My yoke is easy and My burden is light." That is the way to take His burden up. You will find that His burden is always light. Yours is a very heavy one. Happy day if you have exchanged burdens and laid down your loads at His blessed feet to take up His own instead. God wants to rest His workers, and He is too kind to put His burden on hearts that are already bowed down with their own weight of cares.

Are you fearing, fretting or repining?
You can never know God's perfect peace.
On His bosom all your weight reclining.
All your anxious doubts and cares must cease.
Would you know the peace that God has given?
Would you find the very joy of heaven?
Be careful for nothing,
Be prayerful for everything,
Be thankful for anything,
And the peace of God that passeth understanding
Shall keep your mind and heart.

DECEMBER 18.

"The faith of the Son of God" (Gal. ii. 20).

Faith is hindered most of all by what we call "our faith," and fruitless struggles to work out a faith which is but a make-believe and a desperate trying to trust God, which must ever come short of His vast and glorious promises. The truth is that the only faith that is equal to the stupendous promises of God and the measureless needs of our life, is "the faith of God" Himself, the very trust which He will breathe into the heart which intelligently expects Him as its power to believe, as well as its power to love, obey, or perform any other exercise of the new life.

Blessed be His name! He has not given us a chain which reaches within a single link of our poor helpless heart, but that one last link is fatal to all the chain.

191

Nay, the last link, the one that fastens on the human side is as Divine as the link that binds the chain of promise in the heavens. "Have the faith of God," is His great command. "I live by the faith of the Son of God" is the victorious testimony of one who had proved it true.

Lord, teach me to have the faith of the Son of God.

DECEMBER 19.

"God giveth grace unto the humble" (James iv. 6).

One of the marks of highest worth is deep lowliness. The shallow nature, conscious of its weakness and insufficiency, is always trying to advertise itself and make sure of its being appreciated. The strong nature, conscious of its strength, is willing to wait and let its work be made manifest in due time. Indeed, the truest natures are so free from all self-consciousness and self-consideration that their object is not to be appreciated, understood or recompensed, but to accomplish their true mission and fulfil the real work of life.

One of the most suggestive expressions used respecting the Lord Jesus is given by the evangelist John in the thirteenth chapter of His Gospel, where we read, "Jesus, knowing that He came from God, and went to God, riseth from supper and began to wash the disciples' feet." It was because He knew His high dignity and His high destiny that He could stoop to the lowest place and that place could not degrade Him.

God give to us the Divine insignia of heavenly rank, a bowed head, a meek and lowly spirit.

DECEMBER 20.

"That I should be the minister of Jesus Christ to the Gentiles, ministering the Gospel of God" (Rom. xv. 16).

This is a very beautiful and practical conception of missionary work. There is a great difference in being consecrated to our God. We may be consecrated to our work and consecrated to our God. We may be consecrated and fitted to do missionary work, and utterly fail, if He should call us to do something different. But when we are consecrated to Him, we shall be ready for anything He may require of us, and be as well qualified to serve Him by the sick bed of a brother, or even in the secular duties of home, as in standing in the pulpit or leading a soul to Christ.

Paul's conception is holy work, or a special sacrifice, and directly unto Christ, and Christ alone; and he stood as one should stand at the altar of incense, lifting up with holy hands the Gentile nations unto God, and laying all his work like fragrant incense before the throne, pleased only with what would please his Master, and stand the test of His inspection, and the seal of His approval in that glorious day.

This is the spirit of true service.

DECEMBER 21.

"Give us day by day our daily bread" (Luke xi. 3).

It is very hard to live a lifetime at once, or even a year, but it is delightfully easy to live a day at a time. Day by day the manna fell, so day by day we may live upon the heavenly bread, and live out our life for Him. Let us, breath by breath, moment by moment, step by step, abide in Him, and, just as we take care of the days, He will take care of the years.

God has given two precious promises for the days. "As thy days so shall thy strength be," is His ancient covenant, and the literal translation of our Master's parting words to His disciples is, "Lo, I am with you all the days, even unto the end of the age."

Like the little water spider that goes down beneath the waters of the pool enclosed in a bubble of air, and there builds its nest and rears its young, and lives its little life in that bright sphere down beneath the slimy pool, so let us in this dark world shut ourselves in with Christ in the little circle of each returning day, and so abide in Him, breathing the air of heaven and living in His love.

DECEMBER 22.

"My tongue also shall talk of Thy righteousness all the day long" (Ps. lxxi. 24).

It is a simple law of nature, that air always comes in to fill a vacuum. You can produce a draught at any time, by heating the air until it ascends, and then the cold air rushes in to supply its place. And so we can always be filled with the Holy Spirit by providing a vacuum. This breath is dependent upon exhausting the previous breath before you can inhale a fresh one. And so we must empty our hearts of the last breath of the Holy Spirit that we have received, for it becomes exhausted the moment we have received it, and we need a new supply, to prevent spiritual asphyxia.

We must learn the secret of breathing out, as well as breathing in. Now, the breathing in will continue if the other part is rightly done. One of the best ways to make room for the Holy Spirit is to recognize the needs that come into the life as vacuums for Him to fill, and we shall find plenty of needs all around us to be filled, and as we pour out our lives in holy service, He will pour His in--in full measure.

Jesus, empty me and fill me
With Thy fulness to the brim.

DECEMBER 23.

"Out of the spoils won in battles, did they dedicate to maintain the house of the Lord" (I. Chron. xxvi. 27).

Physical force is stored in the bowels of the earth, in the coal mines, which came from the fiery heat that burned up great forests in ancient ages. And so spiritual force is stored in the depths of our being, through the very sufferings which we cannot understand. Some day we shall find that the deliverance we have won from these trials were preparing us to become true "Great Hearts" in life's Pilgrim's Progress, and to lead our fellow pilgrims triumphantly through trial to the city of the King.

But let us never forget that the source of helping other people must be victorious suffering. The whining, murmuring pang never does anybody any good. Paul did not carry a cemetery with him, but a chorus choir of victorious praise, and the harder the trial, the more he trusted and rejoiced, shouting from the very altar of sacrifice, "Yea, and if I be offered upon the service and sacrifice of your faith, I joy and rejoice with you all."

Lord, help me this day to draw strength from all that comes to me.

DECEMBER 24.

"And seekest thou great things for thyself? Seek them not; for behold I will bring evil upon all flesh, saith the Lord; but thy life will I give unto thee for a prey in all places whither thou goest" (Jer. xlv. 5).

A promise given for hard places, and a promise of safety and life in the midst of tremendous pressure, a life for a prey.

194

It may well adjust itself to our own times, which are growing harder as we near the end of the age, and the tribulation times.

What is the meaning of "a life for a prey"? It means a life snatched out of the jaws of the destroyer, as David snatched the lamb from the lion. It means not a place of security, or of removal from the noise of the battle, and the presence of our foes, but it means a table in the midst of our enemies, a shelter from the storm, a fortress amid the foe, a life preserved in the face of continual pressure, Paul's healing when pressed out of measure so that he despaired even of life, Paul's Divine help when the thorn remained, but the power of Christ rested upon him and the grace of Christ was sufficient.

Lord, give me my life for a prey, and in the hardest places help me to-day to be victorious.

DECEMBER 25.

"I bring you glad tidings" (Luke ii. 10).

A Christmas spirit should be a spirit of humanity. Beside that beautiful object lesson on the Manger, the Cradle, and the lowly little child, what Christian heart can ever wish to be proud? It is a spirit of joy. It is right that these should be glad tidings, for, "Behold, I bring you glad tidings of great joy which shall be to all people."

It is a spirit of love. It should be the joy that comes from giving joy to others. The central fact of Christmas is the Christ who loved us, and came to live among us and die for us, and he or she has no right to share its joys who is living for himself or herself alone.

Love is always sacrificial, and so the Christmas spirit will call us to a glad and full surrender, first to God, and then the joyful sacrifice of what we call our own for His glory and the good of others.

The Christmas spirit is a spirit of worship. It finds the Magi at His feet with their gold and frankincense and myrrh. Let it find us there, too.

The Christmas spirit is a spirit of missions. Its glad tidings are for all people.

DECEMBER 26.

"The Spirit that dwelleth in us lusteth to envy" (James iv. 5).

This beautiful passage has been unhappily translated in our Revised Version: "The Spirit that dwelleth in us lusteth to envy." It ought to be, "The Spirit that dwelleth in us loveth us to jealousy." It is the figure of a love that suffers because of its intense regard for the loved object.

The Holy Ghost is so anxious to accomplish in us and for us the highest will of God, and to receive from us the truest love for Christ, our Divine Husband, that He becomes jealous when in any way we disappoint Him, or divide His love with others.

Therefore, it is said in the preceding passage, "Ye adulterers and adulteresses, know ye not that the friendship of the world is enmity with God?"

Oh, shall we grieve so kind a Friend? Shall we disappoint so loving a Husband? Shall we not meet the blessed Holy Spirit with the love He brings us, and give in return our undivided and unbounded affection?

Was there ever a Bridegroom so loving seeking our heart to gain?

DECEMBER 27.

"He sent forth the dove which returned not again unto him" (Gen. viii. 12).

First, we have the dove going forth from the ark, and finding no rest upon the wild and drifting waste of sin and judgment. This represents the Old Testament period, perhaps, when the Holy Ghost visited this sinful world, but could find no resting-place, and went back to the bosom of God.

Next, we have the dove going forth and returning with the olive leaf in her mouth, the symbol and the pledge of peace and reconciliation, the sign that judgment was passed and peace was returning. Surely this may beautifully represent the next stage of the Holy Spirit's manifestation, as going forth in the ministry and death of Jesus Christ, to proclaim reconciliation to a sinful world.

There is a third stage, when, at length, the dove goes forth from the ark and returns no more; but it makes the world its home, and builds its nest amid the habitations of men. This is the third and present stage of the Holy Spirit's blessed work. Let us welcome the Dove to a nest in our hearts.

DECEMBER 28.

"The Holy Ghost, whom God hath given to them that obey Him" (Acts v. 32).

We can only know and prove the fulness of the Spirit as we step out into the larger purposes and plans of Christ for the world.

Perhaps the chief reason why the Holy Spirit has been so limited in His work in the hearts of Christians, is the shameful neglect of the unsaved and

196

unevangelized world by the great majority of the professed followers of Christ. There are millions of professing Christians--and, perhaps, real Christians--in the world, who have never given one real, earnest thought to the evangelization of the heathen world.

God will not give the Holy Spirit in His fulness for the selfish enjoyment of any Christian. His power is a great trust, which we must use for the benefit of others and for the evangelization of the lost and sinful world. Not until the people of God awake to understand His real purpose for the salvation of men, will the Church ever know the fulness of her Pentecost. God's promised power must lie along the line of duty, and as we obey the command, we shall receive His promise in his fulness.

Lord, help me to understand Thy plan.

DECEMBER 29.

"I have not shunned to declare unto you all the counsel of God" (Acts xx. 27).

It is probable that God lets every human being, that crosses our path, meet us, in order that we may have the opportunity of leaving some blessing in his path, and dropping into his heart and life some influence that will draw him nearer to God. It would be blessed, indeed, if we could meet every immortal soul, at last, that we have ever touched in the path of life, and truly say, "I am pure from the blood of all men."

Beloved, is it so? The servant that works in your household; the man that sat beside you in the train; the laborer that wrought for you, and, above all, the members of your household and family, your fellow-laborer in the shop or factory, have you done your best to lead them to Christ?

The early Christians regarded every situation as an opportunity to witness for Christ. Even when brought before kings and governors, it never occurred to them that they were to try to get free, but the Master's message to them was, "It shall turn to you for a testimony." It was simply an occasion to preach to kings and rulers, whom otherwise they could not reach.

DECEMBER 30.

"That God would fulfil in you all the good pleasure of His goodness, and the work of faith with power" (II. Thess. i. 11).

197

Our God is looking to-day for pattern men, and when He gets a true sample, it is very easy to reproduce it in a thousand editions, and multiply it in other lives without limitation.

All the experiences of life come to us as tests, and as we meet them, our loving Father is watching with intense and jealous love, to see us overcome, and if we fail He is deeply disappointed, and our adversary is filled with joy.

We are a gazing-stock continually for angels and principalities, and every step we take is critical and decisive for something in our eternal future.

When Abraham went forth that morning to Mount Moriah, it was an hour of solemn probation, and when he came back he was one of God's tested men, with the stamp of His eternal approbation. God could say, "I know him, that he will do judgment and justice, that the Lord may bring upon Abraham all that He hath spoken."

God is looking for such men to-day. Lord, help me to be such an one.

DECEMBER 31.

"I pray not that Thou shouldst take them out of the world, but that Thou shouldst keep them from the evil" (John xvii. 15).

He wants us here for some higher purpose than mere existence. That purpose is nothing else than to represent Him to the world, to be the messengers of His Gospel and His will to men, and by our lives to exhibit to them the true life, and teach them how to live it themselves.

He is representing us yonder, and our one business is to represent Him here. We are just as truly sent into this world to represent Him as if we had gone to China as the ambassador of the American Government.

While engaged in the secular affairs of life, it is simply that we may represent Him there, carry on His business, and have means to use for His affairs. He came here from another realm, and with a special message, and when His work was done He was called to go home to His Father's dwelling-place and His own.

Lord, help me to worthily represent Thee.

And carry music in our heart
Through busy street and wrangling mart;
Plying our daily task with busier feet,
Because our souls a heavenly strain repeat

Made in United States
Orlando, FL
10 December 2022

25974765R00125